TACTICAL
COMMUNICATION

Law enforcement tools for successful
encounters with people from poverty,
middle class, and wealth.

aha! Process, Inc. ▪ P.O. Box 727 ▪ Highlands, TX 77562-0727
(800) 424-9484 ▪ (281) 426-5300 ▪ Fax: (281) 426-5600
Website: www.ahaprocess.com

Library of Congress Cataloging-in-Publication Data

Jodi R. Pfarr
Tactical Communication: Law enforcement tools for successful encounters with people from poverty, middle class, and wealth.
111 pp.
References p. 109-111
ISBN 13: 978-1-934583-31-9
ISBN 10: 1-934583-31-6

Library of Congress Control Number: 2008940549

1. Education   2. Sociology   3. Title

Copy editing by Jesse Conrad
Book design by Paula Nicolella
Cover design by Naylor Design, Inc.

Printed in the United States of America

Grateful acknowledgment is made for permission to reprint copyrighted material, including numerous charts and graphs, from *A Framework for Understanding Poverty* by Dr. Ruby K. Payne, *Bridges Out of Poverty* by Dr. Ruby K. Payne, Philip E. DeVol, and Terie Dreussi Smith, and *Getting Ahead in a Just-Gettin'-By World* by Philip E. DeVol.

TACTICAL
COMMUNICATION

Law enforcement tools for successful
encounters with people from poverty,
middle class, and wealth.

Jodi R. Pfarr

Acknowledgements

I would like to thank the St. Paul Police Department for its support of this project. In particular, Chief John M. Harrington and Sergeant Cheryl D. Indehar, whose commitment to the development of this content made this book possible. I also thank Chief William K. Finney (Ret.) and Deputy Chief Thomas Smith for helping us begin this process. In addition, the following sworn officers deserve special thanks for their willingness to meet with me on a regular basis and share their invaluable insight and knowledge: Sheriff Dave Schleve (Ret.), Sheriff Toby Wishard, Sergeant Jack Serier, Sergeant Joe Strong, Sergeant Rutha DeJesus, Officer Timothy Bradley, Officer Darryl Hunter, Officer Errol Johnson, Officer Lucia Wroblewski, and Officer Xiong Yang.

To Dr. Ruby K. Payne, Philip E. DeVol, and Terie Dreussi Smith, co-authors of *Bridges Out of Poverty*, I thank you for your contributions to the area of understanding the different economic classes and building sustainable communities. Your powerful work and the shared language you provided is the foundation for many of the tools and strategies within this book. Thank you, Dr. Payne, for your continued support and the encouragement to write this book. A large amount of gratitude goes to the aha! Process publications team for their hard work and patience.

Finally, I want to thank everyone who works in law enforcement for the challenging job that they do every day. It is my hope that this book will help them reduce the challenges they face in their jobs and increase the rewards.

v

TABLE OF CONTENTS

Introduction

This book is written for law enforcement. Law enforcement personnel have a difficult job as they are continuously called upon to work within many communities of different economic status. When people's economic status influences their access to our societal system, it affects the experience those people have in society. That experience shapes how many things, including law enforcement, are viewed and treated. Officers who have worked in all three economic communities (poverty, middle, and wealthy classes) can testify to being viewed and treated differently within each of these communities. The deeper the understanding law enforcement personnel have of these differences, the safer they can keep themselves and the communities they serve.

Law enforcement is particularly challenging because officers are constantly called upon to work outside of the economic classes they are used to. When law enforcement workers, like anyone else, see things operate in a way that does not reflect their own experience, it is hard for them to make sense of the situation. When people see something they cannot understand or make sense of, human nature is to react to it. Reacting means the officer is no longer in control, no longer choosing what happens next. Any law enforcement worker will tell you that is a dangerous place to be.

This book is not meant to justify or judge the behaviors one might witness, nor is it attempting to present a solution for the problem of a societal system that provides different degrees of access based on economic status. This book is a tool for law enforcement; like any other tool on your belt, you will decide when to pick it up and utilize it and when to leave it be.

Throughout the book you will find mental models, usually in the form of illustrations, that introduce key points. You will see that the first chapters share understanding about the different economic communities and individual behaviors and attitudes within those communities. This is very useful information for officers working directly with individuals or within different economic communities. As officers advance in their careers, the job requires them to gain more of a community-wide perspective. The last chapter of this book focuses on how to use this information in a more systemic manner.

I would like to thank all law enforcement personnel for the work each of you does. I hope you find this book helpful.

—Jodi Pfarr

KEY POINTS:

1) This book is written for law enforcement. Law enforcement personnel are often required to serve economically diverse communities; therefore, the more officers understand what they are encountering, the less they will react to particular situations—and that means they can better stay in control. Staying in control allows an officer the luxury of choosing the next action, a choice that ultimately keeps law enforcement personnel and the community safe.

2) Communities are diverse in many ways: age, gender, ethnicity, race, sexual orientation, and economic status, for example, vary by community and within each community. All types of diversity affect communities and should be discussed. This book focuses on economic diversity between and within communities.

3) This book focuses on generational poverty, generational middle class, and generational wealth. Economic classes can be split into many different groups, but if we want to compare/contrast the classes in order to further understand them, using the three categories listed above simplifies our task.

4) This work is based on patterns. All patterns have exceptions. People often choose not to talk about the different ways economic groups operate because they fear being accused of stereotyping. I am not asserting that if you live in one community or the other you are guaranteed to be or act a certain way—that would be absurd. Still, it is equally absurd to state that no differences exist between the different economic communities. We must have the courage to start to talk about the differences in a way that is respectful to all. This book attempts to provide law enforcement

personnel with a better understanding of patterns they witness and experience on the job. This understanding will help law enforcement personnel keep themselves and the community safer. I trust that law enforcement workers will not use the information to profile people, but will use it to better understand and relate to the events and people they encounter in their professional capacities. I also hope this book will help readers understand their experience of the societal system at large with regard to economic status.

5) Generational poverty, middle class, and wealth mean that individuals have been in that class for two generations or more. People in a generational class are more likely to exhibit the patterns associated with that class than are people whose families haven't been in it for two generations or more.

6) Situational poverty, middle class, and wealth mean that one spends only a period of one's life in that class. For example, if you grew up in middle class and maintained middle class status into adulthood, but then experienced poverty due to an illness or other mitigating factor, this would be considered situational poverty. You would not bring the same lenses and mindset to the experience of poverty as would someone who has never experienced anything else.

7) Poverty, middle class, and wealth are all relative. The 2008 Current Population Survey (conducted jointly by the Bureau of Labor Statistics and the Census Bureau) tells us that a household with an annual income of $100,000 or more is in the top 20% of American households as ranked by income, which leads the other 80% of people to consider them rich; however, if you asked households making that amount if they are rich, few would say that they are. They would think of friends who make more money as a basis for comparison. The point is that perception of economic class is relative.

8) Individuals bring with them the hidden rules of the class in which they were raised.

9) Law enforcement, schools, social services, and businesses tend to operate from middle class norms and use the hidden rules of middle class.

10) In order to move from one economic class to another, an individual must often give up relationships for achievement for a period of time.

11) For law enforcement personnel to be perceived as good leaders, they must understand the hidden rules in operation and translate the law in a meaningful manner.

Chapter One

MENTAL MODELS OF POVERTY, MIDDLE CLASS, AND WEALTH

Mental models are pictures, drawings, or stories that communicate a lot of information in a small amount of time. Mental models are frequently used in law enforcement and the military. They not only help deliver a lot of information in a short time, they can also assist in understanding the content. When a serious crime is committed the police department will often get a sketch of the person who committed the crime and/or map out the scene. They don't stop at gathering a long, verbal description of the person or crime scene; no, a mental model is created. The mental model helps communicate a lot of information in a short time.

Every one of us already holds mental models of what poverty, middle class, and wealth look like. Some of our mental models of poverty come from our parents or grandparents who to this day save paper bags and rubber bands as a result of their experiences during the Great Depression. Some of us get our mental models of poverty from media. Some of us did not have strong mental models of poverty until we came to work and saw a family in poverty with people working two and three jobs and still barely getting by. Or perhaps the first family in poverty we saw wasn't working at all. Some of us have very strong mental models of poverty because we grew up there. However or wherever we developed our mental models, this chapter attempts to set forth a mental model that incorporates all of the ideas.

Think of an adult in generational poverty (not situational poverty), and follow that adult around for an entire day. What does that person spend time doing? Do the same for a middle class person and a wealthy person.

The circles that follow in this chapter represent average days in the lives of people in poverty, middle class, and wealth. It is worth noting that the mental model used to represent people in poverty was generated by people currently living in poverty, the middle class circle by people in middle class, and the wealthy circle by someone in wealth. Of course, everybody's circle looks a little different—one item may take up more time in one's circle than in another's—but the basic components are generally the same.

A MENTAL MODEL OF POVERTY

Let's analyze the circles. We'll begin by looking at the poverty circle. What does transportation look like in poverty? Public transit, walking, bicycling, an older, broken-down car, or if you have been very successful in an illicit trade, a decked-out ride. Transportation is generally unreliable at best, as is often the case with housing, as well.

Mental Model of Poverty

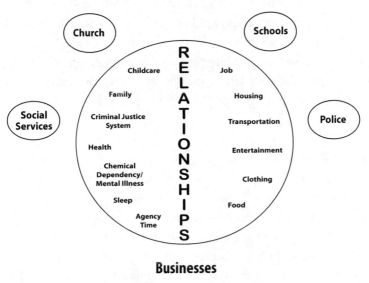

Businesses

Pawn Shop	Fast Food
Liquor Store	Check Cashing
Corner Store	Temp Services
Rent-to-Own	Payday Loans
Laundromat	Used Car Lots
Dollar Store	

Source: *Bridges Out of Poverty: Strategies for Professionals and Communities Workbook* (2006)

The first home address law enforcement receives for someone who lives in poverty is rarely the correct address. An officer will have to go two or three moves further to catch up with someone. Such things as mental illness and chemical dependency are not always seen in poverty, but any officer will tell you that they tend to be observed at higher rates overall in poverty than in the other two classes.

Incarceration rates are similar. Not every person from poverty experiences incarceration in the criminal justice system, but go to your local city or county jail or state prison and you'll find that the trend is people from poverty are represented at a higher rate than are those from middle class, and at a much higher rate than are people who come from wealth. Why this discrepancy exists is not the focus of this book, but it is a question worth raising and worthy of further analysis elsewhere.

As we look at the poverty circle, we begin to see that the circle is not always stable, and tasks take a longer time to accomplish. In poverty you take the pile of dirty laundry, gather up the kids, and go down to a Laundromat. At the Laundromat you wash the clothes, watch the kids, and unless you have a lot of money, you rarely get the clothes completely dry. Then you run for the bus but miss it, and it is the last bus of the day, so now you call back to the neighborhood to someone who has a car. Remember, it is the only ride in the neighborhood, so the driver has to drop off four other people before picking you up. Gas prices being what they are, you'd better have some gas money. The ride finally arrives; you load up everything and pull away, only to have the car stall out at the second stop sign because it is an unreliable car. Tasks take a longer time in poverty.

We begin to see that living in poverty is about survival, about getting today's needs met. When your life is about survival, it quickly becomes about today and now—not next year, not even tomorrow; it is all about today and surviving this moment. This point cannot be emphasized enough. In generational poverty it is all about the *right now.* There is often no grand future story, no picture of what you look like in the future. More time is spent focusing on surviving the moment, which leaves less time to focus on the future. Therefore, in poverty, you will generally hear less talk about going to college or buying a house (future events) than you will hear in middle class.

Officers, how many times have you arrested people who, once they got to jail, seemed very surprised they were there, even though you had seen them making decisions long ago that would lead to jail? A young man in generational poverty (12–14 years of age) once told me he was "getting the heck out." When I asked him what that looked like, he stared at me. I stared back. It was obvious he had never really thought about, nor had anyone talked to him about, what "getting the heck out" looked like. Eventually he gave me an answer I am pretty sure the media fed him: "I'm gonna be a rock star!"

Although he had a desire for some type of change, he had no future story of what this change would look like. This is where police have a rare opportunity and power. I know most days it doesn't feel that way, but do not underestimate the impact you, as a law enforcement official, have on each one of these circles. You can give that child a new future story. I travel the nation and present this information. I continuously have people from generational poverty in my audiences say they never would have "made it out" had it not been for a key relationship with someone. Often that someone is a police officer, teacher, or social worker.

When one lacks a strong future story to focus on during a difficult moment, one will often react based on the immediacy of the situation. When an officer states, "Do this or you go to jail," the reaction is often, "So what?" When one's life is all about *right now*, that statement is of little consequence; however, when one is focused on the future, as many middle class people are, then one will process that statement in terms of the future. As in, "Wait a minute. If I don't do this, I go to jail. That means the neighbors see me get arrested, and my partner or spouse has to bail me out, and then I have to deal with a lawyer … " The future ramifications outweigh the moment at hand. We will talk more about this concept in the next chapter. The piece to note for now is that because people in poverty are busy trying to survive, life often becomes about the right now, not a future story.

OBTAINING ASSISTANCE

In the poverty circle, "agency time" refers to the time one spends at different agencies and organizations obtaining various forms of assistance with surviving. In many communities, social service, educational, criminal justice, and healthcare organizations *do not* work closely with one another, even though many or all of the organizations may be working with the same family. This bureaucratic, compartmentalized way of doing things often has people in poverty running from one place to another to receive services. When the organizations do not work together, it can actually encourage individuals to manipulate the system. When a person from poverty encounters the first organization in the morning, that person nods and smiles and gives the answers the organization wants to hear in order to get what is needed to survive and to be allowed to leave. Then that person goes to the next organization in the afternoon and again nods and smiles and gives them the answers they want to hear in order to get what is needed and to be allowed to leave. By the time people get to their third organization of the day, they are done nodding and smiling. They just tell the organization what is wanted, demand it, and then leave. Often these large systems are not set up to hold anyone accountable or to be accountable to any entities other than themselves.

How is a given social service organization set up? Who sits on its board? Who writes its rules? To whom is it accountable? Rarely are police, people in poverty, or others who are directly affected by social service organizations being asked for input or to be involved within the organization in a powerful way. Ultimately, in many of our communities, we have created organizations that act like silos with police and people who utilize the services running between them. For this reason criminal justice, educational, social service, and healthcare organizations must be willing to work much more closely with each other, learn from one another, and be accountable to one another.

A MENTAL MODEL OF MIDDLE CLASS

Let's look at the middle class mental model. In middle class you will often see a career instead of a J-O-B. A career is something you want to hold onto for a while, something on which you can build. A career usually provides the middle class household with health benefits, vacation, sick time, and a livable wage. A livable wage means you're going to be able to get your basic needs met (food, clothing, and housing). In the United States, $10–12 per hour is the most widely accepted definition of a livable wage. Of course, the amount that is considered livable varies depending on where you are and how much it costs to live there. In Minneapolis/St. Paul, a livable wage is currently $14–16 per hour. In San Diego it is $20–22 per hour.

Mental Model of Middle Class

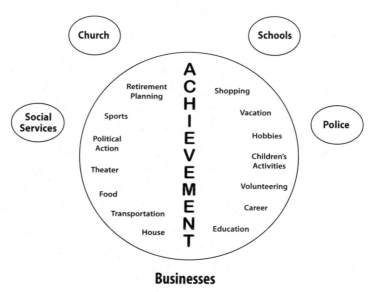

Source: *Bridges Out of Poverty: Strategies for Professionals and Communities Workbook* (2006)

A livable wage is a major contributor to household stability. Your financial needs are met for today, and that frees you up to focus on the future. How far into the future you can focus often depends a great deal upon the amount of disposable income you earn. If your household only makes $2–4 above the livable wage, then you might only be planning two to four months into the future. Still, if your household is making $10–15 dollars above the livable wage, then you may be looking 30 years into the future, planning for your retirement, saving for the kids' future education, or saving for a hobby like a boat or a cabin in a good hunting area.

A career also gives a person an identity that is recognized by society. Go to a middle class party, and once you have a drink in hand—because middle class is often concerned that you have one—what is one of the first questions people ask?

"WHAT DO YOU DO?"

If you say, "I'm a police officer," (or social worker or teacher), people often respond with, "Oh, that must be so rewarding," or, "Hey, I got a ticket the other day. Can you … " In a later chapter we will discuss family patterns and analyze how having an identity that society at large acknowledges affects parenting.

TRANSPORTATION

Middle class transportation is generally reliable—you find SUVs, minivans, etc., and sometimes one household will have multiple vehicles. As we analyze the middle class and poverty circles, we begin to see how things like transportation affect daily life. In middle class people jump into cars that will definitely start, drive to the grocery store, don't worry that they won't be able to afford groceries (their careers' livable wages in most cases guarantee that the money is in a checking account), purchase their groceries, put them into the reliable vehicles, and head home again. In middle class one's basic needs are usually met, so time and energy are given to other activities. One may choose to get involved with a union, go back to school, pick up a new (or another) hobby, get the kids involved in various activities, or get politically active. The point is that financial resources can help bring stability to the circle. This financial stability is a major element that contributes to one's ability to have a strong future story. It can also help one to contain life's problems so that they don't have an impact on other aspects of one's life.

When transportation is lost in middle class, meaning a vehicle breaks down or is damaged in an accident, the owner of the vehicle often has access to credit. A person in middle class whose vehicle is out of service takes a credit card to the car rental agency and rents a car until the first one can be repaired or replaced. A middle class person may have a relationship with another person who also lives in a financially stable circle. If a neighbor has three cars, people in middle class may be able to borrow one until they can reestablish their own transportation. Thus the problem of losing one's transportation is contained to just that area of the circle—transportation.

In contrast, people in poverty often do not have access to credit, nor do they have family and friends in financially stable places. Consequently, in poverty, when transportation is lost, the next thing affected is your job. Though you try to catch rides to work, you end up being late one too many times and lose the job. If the job is lost, housing is the next thing that falls into jeopardy. This is how, in the absence of certain resources, one of life's problems can quickly expand to affect numerous other areas of one's life.

It should be noted that as this book is being written, many middle class families are feeling their financial stability slipping away. Due to the rising cost of living, many middle class families are finding it harder to maintain stability within the circle.

A MENTAL MODEL OF WEALTH

In the wealthy circle your family was financially secure when you were born into it, or you've made so much money in your lifetime that you and your children's circle, maybe even your grandchildren's circle, is financially secure. Here it is neither about a J-O-B nor a career; in the wealthy circle, the focus is on managing the money you have, ensuring that your money generates more money, and keeping up connections with others that will assist you in maintaining the status you currently hold.

Mental Model of Wealth

Businesses

Private Yachting, Horse, and Tennis Clubs
High-End Luxury Merchants

Exclusive Dining Boutiques and Specialty Stores

Source: *Bridges Out of Poverty: Strategies for Professionals and Communities Workbook* (2006)

In wealth life's problems can not only be contained, they are often dealt with by other people. Financial resources are available to compensate people who ensure your basic needs are met. In other words, you have people whose job it is to make sure you are taken care of. People from wealth may sometimes relate to law enforcement workers in the same way they relate to their hired help. In their view an officer is there to assist them with getting their needs met and nothing else.

APPLICATIONS IN LAW ENFORCEMENT

Law enforcement workers do not have the luxury of choosing who they want to work with. They are expected to be successful with all citizens. Thus the more officers understand about the people they come into contact with, the more effective they can be. Be careful here not to confuse understanding with justifying or promoting. This book does not attempt to justify or endorse any particular behaviors observed in wealth, middle class, or poverty. The hope is that the book will share an understanding that enables law enforcement personnel to choose their responses carefully and avoid reactionary responses to unfamiliar situations. If one has a reactionary response, it is often perceived as a judgmental response. After all, it is human nature to judge something that is not understood. When officers are perceived as being judgmental, they quickly find themselves with uncooperative civilians. To understand—not to justify or to promote, but to understand—is the first step toward choosing each of your responses. The ability to choose means officers stay in control, which builds relationships with civilians, which in turn keeps the officers safer and makes the job easier.

As we look further at the mental models, we see that the businesses in the communities are different. Businesses present in poverty are focused on survival: pawn shops, check cashing and payday loans, rent-to-own, Laundromats, etc. In middle class the stores tend to be more specific and sell things that appeal to people whose outlook is future-based: realtors, jewelry stores, antique shops, insurance agencies, travel agencies, and so on. If we recall that a livable wage contributes to a more stabilized circle, we must then ask, "Does the community offer as many livable wage jobs as there are people in poverty?" If people in poverty cannot access jobs in the community that pay a livable wage, chances are that poverty will grow. This directly affects police departments.

DRIVING FORCES

Another element that has a direct impact on civilian-police relations in the different communities is the primary driving force in each community. In poverty the driving force is *relationships;* in middle class it is *achievement;* in wealth it is *connections.*

RELATIONSHIPS

When your world is about surviving, you need other people to help you survive; therefore, relationships affect everything in the poverty circle. This is why the word is written in the middle of the circle. Most law enforcement workers have stories about people who would not provide police with information about another person because of their relationship to that person. The person unwilling to talk would rather go to jail than "rat out" or "snitch on" a friend. Law enforcement personnel who have relationships with people in poverty can attest to the huge advantage those relationships lend to gathering evidence, getting citizens to cooperate, and ultimately solving crimes.

Take for example an officer who has worked in the same community for more than 20 years, who always treats people in poverty with respect, who holds them accountable in a respectful manner, who takes the time to gain trust through relationships, and who has great moments of success because of it. When this officer goes to a house and explains to a mother that her son is wanted and simply states, "Mrs. Olson, you know me. I promise I will treat your boy well if you turn him over to me. If I have to call for backup, or if another officer has to take him in, I can't promise that," Mrs. Olson calls for her son and tells him to go with the officer. The badge itself doesn't necessarily get you respect in a neighborhood in poverty; relationships of mutual respect will.

TOOL:
- **Power in poverty ≠ the badge**
- **Relationships in poverty = power and respect**
- **Power and respect = more cooperative citizens and increased personal safety**

Building and maintaining relationships can help you as a law enforcement worker stay safe and be effective; it can also help your fellow officers. You can enter a neighborhood in poverty in a disrespectful manner and survive—it is done daily. But what if your fellow officer has to return to the same house on the next shift? What kind of treatment will your colleague receive now that the person in poverty personally associates the uniform with disrespect?

A relationship of mutual respect does not mean an officer has to "kiss ass" or "be nicer" in one neighborhood but not in another. A relationship of mutual respect begins with simply understanding the community you are in and conducting yourself based on that understanding, rather than upon judgment. For example, if a wealthy person comes to a middle class party, looks disgusted at the quality of the food and beverages, and is frustrated with the lack of wait staff, many middle class people at the party will take offense to that response. Why? Because the wealthy person was not operating out of an understanding of how a middle class party works; rather, the wealthy person made a judgment based only upon his or her experience of how a party should be and acted on that judgment. People don't want others from a different class to tell them their class is inferior. This is as true in middle class as it is in poverty, as well as in wealth. Similarly, an officer from middle class who enters a situation in poverty and responds judgmentally will also receive a negative reaction. Perhaps you have found yourself in a situation like this on the job, a situation in which you accidentally offended people because you didn't share the same hidden rules. Situations like this are easier to avoid if officers build their understanding of the patterns of the different economic classes—beginning with the patterns of their own economic class.

ACHIEVEMENT

People in middle class are interested in maintaining stability and hope to gain more stability in the future. As a result, achievement is highly valued. In middle class, if you buy a small starter home and eight years later buy a bigger house, you congratulate yourself. Go back to school and earn a degree? Great! Your favorite team takes it all the way and wins? What could be better? Middle class loves achievement.

Within the United States there are some communities or cultures that absolutely nurture relationships more than other communities or cultures. Officers have noted as they work in many different communities and across many different cultures that some will "take care of each other" more than other communities or cultures. If middle class people feel they live in a community that cares for its members very deeply, or they are from a culture that emphasizes relationships more than others, then they would want to write "relationships" right next to "achievement" in the circle. However, these people will spend a lifetime learning to balance the two driving forces.

People will always give back to their communities or cultures, but rarely do they allow that community or culture to overtake the stability of the circle. This balancing can take a lot of time and energy. For example, should you allow people to stay at your house? Sure! As one who understands the importance of relationships, that is something that is expected. But allowing too many people to stay in your house can put the quality of life in the home—and even the housing itself—in jeopardy, which is unacceptable because it disrupts the stability of your circle and undercuts your ability to achieve more in the future.

In generational poverty, no matter the region or culture, relationships are dominant. For example, in poverty you may hear something like this: "What do you mean you can't watch my kids tonight because you have to study for a GED test? I've watched your kids a hundred times!" This is a relationship-based perspective that doesn't take into account other driving forces—the desire to achieve a passing score on the GED, for example. But, if relationships are dominant, that person is likely to put down the books for the GED and watch the kids.

CONNECTIONS

In wealth, political, social, and financial connections are essential to maintaining one's status. "Knowing the right people" can in fact ensure that your family's status is maintained for generations to come. Many officers have stories about pulling over an extremely wealthy person and being scolded, as in, "Do you know who I am? Do you know *who I know?*"

A police department once participated in a local charity event by having a fake jail and "arresting" people. Then others in the community could make a donation to the cause and release their friends who had been arrested. The department approached a man from generational wealth and asked if he would participate. He hesitated, but agreed on the condition that the chief of police be the "arresting officer." Just as people in poverty rely heavily on relationships to survive, and people in middle class rely heavily on achievement to maintain stability, people in wealth rely on political, social, and financial connections to maintain their wealth and social status.

The mental models we've discussed are intended to further our understanding of patterns that law enforcement personnel observe on the job. In order to truly deepen that understanding, we have to be honest and talk about what we have seen, whether it is "politically correct" or not. We must also be willing to admit that, like all humans, we tend to judge things we don't understand. But this kind of judgment, without seeking first to understand, can make for a long and stressful career. We must have the courage to discuss class in an honest manner, without pulling punches, while maintaining the level of professionalism and respect for the people we serve that the badge represents. If we do not gain understanding, we will act based on uninformed judgments. That not only puts law enforcement personnel at risk, it also destroys the potential for learning on both sides of the encounter.

Once, while I was presenting this material to a large group, a person asked me, "When I do a home visit in poverty, every once in awhile there is a $75,000 Lexus in the driveway. Can you help me understand that?" If we look back at the mental models, the answer to that question becomes clearer. If you obtain reliable transportation in poverty, does your status in the community increase or decrease? Tenfold, it increases, especially with a luxury car! Being able to provide transportation in poverty is a valuable bartering tool. Perhaps you haven't established a relationship with that person in the community who fixes plumbing. Well, now if your plumbing breaks, you can get it fixed, because there will come a time when the plumber and his family will need a ride. In poverty repair services are often unaffordable, so you must know how to do it yourself, have a relationship with someone who knows, or have something like transportation to barter.

After hearing that example, another audience member will usually ask, "But isn't there a good chance that the expensive transportation will be lost or destroyed?" When one has a strong future story, that is certainly a concern. However, when you are living for this moment, and that expensive transportation causes your status in the community to increase, you are getting more needs met, your family has reliable transportation for the now, and it is worthwhile. Someone else once asked, "OK, why not get the $6,000 reliable transportation? Why the $75,000 car?"

I responded, "Think of the American Dream as a pie; it consists of different slices. In generational poverty some of our communities are starting to let go of some of those slices. Housing? Probably not going to get it unless someone passes it down. Education? Some communities are starting to let it go. Transportation is one of the slices of the American Dream you can still get. Why not put whipped cream and strawberries on that slice? Things are very different in middle class. People in middle class still want, and believe they can achieve, many of those slices: education, vacation, transportation, career, etc. So the prevailing wisdom is that you don't put whipped cream and strawberries on just one slice because that may hinder you from achieving the other slices in the future."

A professor from a major university heard this and said, "OK, I understand the $75,000 vehicle. I understand why that and not a $6,000 vehicle. But this is what I don't understand: Why not focus your attention on the education slice of the pie? Why not put aside the transportation slice and focus on education, something that can pay off for you in the future?"

The key word there was *future*. Though there are numerous reasons, the biggest is that education is future-based; it does not necessarily help with the right now. Another reason is that you often need finances, time, and transportation in order to further your education, and so have to work to secure those slices first. Some people in the community may support you in furthering your education, but there will also be those who will challenge you and ask, "Who do you think you are?" The payoffs of education are not immediately visible. If I drive through the community in an extremely nice car, that gets noticed. If I drive through the community with my master's degree, it is not as noticeable; it could even attract negative comments and criticism.

HOUSING

Floor Plan of the House

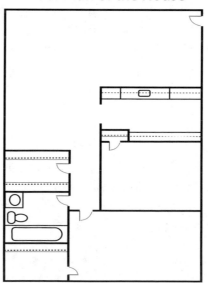

Many factors within the community directly affect policing. Still, it is common for communities to point the finger at only one part of the system and blame it for all of the community's problems. We point at the school system and say things like, "If you just learned to teach better, we would not have these low test scores." To police we say, "If you did your job better, we wouldn't have these increasing crime rates." To social services we say, "If you just did what we pay you for, we wouldn't have poverty in the first place." And so on.

While it is true that all professions should continue to strive to be as effective as they can be, we must also look at other factors in the community that directly affect our jobs. At the beginning of this section there is a mental model of a two-bedroom house. Envision that two-bedroom house in the generational poverty neighborhood. How many people tend to live there? What do things tend to look like? How does this affect the community? How does it directly affect your job? Now imagine a two-bedroom house in a generational middle class neighborhood. How many people tend to live there? How do things tend to look? How does this affect the community? How does this directly affect your job? Finally, imagine a two-bedroom house in wealth. How many people tend to live there? What do things tend to look like? Is it a main residence, a vacation home, or perhaps servants' quarters? How does this affect the community? How does it affect your job?

It should be noted that in all of these exercises I am asking for what things "tend to look like." Please keep in mind key point 4 from page xi regarding naming general patterns as opposed to making generalizations.

Criminological research shows that the more non-blood relatives who live in a house, the higher the chances of physical and sexual abuse occurring in that house. The housing situation in your community absolutely affects your job. If someone in your community works full-time and earns $7 per hour, that person makes about $1,213 per month before taxes. If that person spends 35% of the monthly income on housing (a standard banker's recommendation to people in middle class), then that person can afford to spend $424 per month on a place to live. $424 per month means that most of the available housing is unaffordable; consequently, people in poverty often share living space. There is no question that this affects the jobs of law enforcement personnel.

Another crucial difference dictated by the environment at home can be illustrated like this: In middle class, when a coworker is driving you crazy or citizens are simply getting on your last nerve, you often have access to various forms of relief from the situation. In the moment of the other person testing your patience, you may be able to look at that person and think, "In two weeks I go on vacation!" A future story may pull you through the moment. Or, because you have a good housing situation, you might go home to a quiet room and get on the computer, you might get a drink from the refrigerator, watch TV, take a hot bubble bath, pick up a tool in the garage, or put on the gloves and work the heavy bag to beat some tension out. The point is that in middle class the house is often conducive to taking a break. One may have to wait for the kids to go to bed before it is truly conducive, but usually, at some point in the evening, it is.

Dealing with frustrating people, of course, is not unique to middle class. In poverty you might have a coworker driving you crazy or a social worker who is insane, and you want the same thing anyone wants—to take a break. But because there are often many occupants, houses in poverty aren't very relaxing places to take a break. For example, you don't want to lock the bathroom door for more than five minutes because someone will need to use the bathroom soon and will start banging on the door. In poverty all the physical space is needed and/or occupied by many people, so other methods of creating personal space are used. Entertainment with an audio component is a popular option. Many kids will come home and put on a headset blaring loudly to drown out everything and everyone else in the house. Adults will put the music up loud or become absorbed in a movie or TV show. Using entertainment to escape is one way to create a break for oneself in poverty, since the busy environment of the house is not conducive. Often there is no future story with a vacation in it, so one gets through the tyranny of the moment by escaping into entertainment. Law enforcement personnel and social workers often ask about the shelves full of DVDs and VHS tapes sometimes seen in households in poverty. Those purchases are similar to the purchases people in middle class make at places like Bath and Body Works, Best Buy, etc. All of these personal comfort and entertainment purchases give one a "break," a sense of escape. In poverty there is rarely a big vacation to Hawaii, but one can escape through a movie. Such substances as food, tobacco, alcohol, and illegal drugs can also provide a sense of relief, break, or escape from the moment.

CONCLUSION

In this chapter we analyzed mental models of generational poverty, middle class, and wealth. We saw that the three circles look different, contain different businesses, and are populated by people with different views and patterns. Law enforcement is a hard job because one must find ways to work effectively with every community. Affordable housing and access to livable wage jobs are just two of many factors that directly affect communities and thus affect law enforcement jobs. The better law enforcement personnel are able to understand the hard things they must witness in all three communities, the better they can stay in control. This control allows an officer to choose the next move—a much safer option than reacting to a situation without understanding it. Law enforcement personnel have to hold each member of each community accountable. They cannot lower or raise the expectations because to do so would undermine the rule of law on which this country was built. The more that law enforcement personnel understand about each of the three communities we discuss in this book, the more effective they can be in serving all citizens.

Chapter Two

HIDDEN RULES

Hidden rules are the rules by which groups operate without ever clearly stating that the rules exist. Different regions, age groups, genders, and countries operate according to different sets of hidden rules. The hidden rules of economic class were first identified by Dr. Ruby Payne in her book *A Framework for Understanding Poverty*. In the United States, the Southern States have different hidden rules than the Northern States, the East Coast operates differently than the West Coast, and the mainland is different than the islands. I recall the first time I traveled to the Hawaiian Islands for work; upon deplaning I was immediately hugged and kissed. This is contrary to the hidden rules of the Midwest, where one hidden rule is that you don't hug and kiss strangers!

The table on the next two pages is from *Bridges Out of Poverty*. It describes the hidden rules surrounding many common issues in poverty, middle class, and wealth.

Hidden Rules Among Classes	POVERTY
POSSESSIONS	People.
MONEY	To be used, spent.
PERSONALITY	Is for entertainment. Sense of humor is highly valued.
SOCIAL EMPHASIS	Social inclusion of people he/she likes.
FOOD	Key question: Did you have enough? Quantity important.
CLOTHING	Clothing valued for individual style and expression of personality.
TIME	Present most important. Decisions made for moment based on feelings or survival.
EDUCATION	Valued and revered as abstract but not as reality.
DESTINY	Believes in fate. Cannot do much to mitigate chance.
LANGUAGE	Casual register. Language is about survival.
FAMILY STRUCTURE	Tends to be matriarchal.
WORLD VIEW	Sees world in terms of local setting.
LOVE	Love and acceptance conditional, based upon whether individual is liked.
DRIVING FORCES	Survival, relationships, entertainment.
HUMOR	About people and sex.

MIDDLE CLASS	WEALTH
Things.	One-of-a-kind objects, legacies, pedigrees.
To be managed.	To be conserved, invested.
Is for acquisition and stability. Achievement is highly valued.	Is for connections. Financial, political, social connections are highly valued.
Emphasis is on self-governance and self-sufficiency.	Emphasis is on social exclusion.
Key question: Did you like it? Quality important.	Key question: Was it presented well? Presentation important.
Clothing valued for its quality and acceptance into norm of middle class. Label important.	Clothing valued for its artistic sense and expression. Designer important.
Future most important. Decisions made against future ramifications.	Traditions and history most important. Decisions made partially on basis of tradition and decorum.
Crucial for climbing success ladder and making money.	Necessary tradition for making and maintaining connections.
Believes in choice. Can change future with good choices now.	Noblesse oblige.
Formal register. Language is about negotiation.	Formal register. Language is about networking.
Tends to be patriarchal.	Depends on who has money.
Sees world in terms of national setting.	Sees world in terms of international view.
Love and acceptance conditional and based largely upon achievement.	Love and acceptance conditional and related to social standing and connections.
Work, achievement.	Financial, political, social connections.
About situations.	About social faux pas.

Source: *Bridges Out of Poverty,* Payne, DeVol, Smith (2006)

The unspoken cues or habits of a group are often revealed when someone from outside the group moves in or when someone from the group moves out. In small, rural churches there are many hidden rules in play. One is that certain families have their own pews, so you shouldn't sit there. Members of the congregation might not even realize that there is a rule in play until a visitor to the church sits down smack dab in the middle of the Johnson family's pew. Only when a hidden rule is broken do we become conscious of the rule itself. Some important hidden rules of which law enforcement personnel should be aware are printed at the beginning of this chapter. These hidden rules are based on economic class.

Because law enforcement officers will come into contact with all economic groups, it will assist them a great deal if they understand the hidden rules used by the people they are serving. With understanding comes the ability to know your surroundings and choose the behavior you feel will be most successful. Once we learn to identify the hidden rules in play within different economic communities, we must then be willing to understand the hidden rules of different age groups, ethnic groups, and genders, to name a few.

FOOD

Officers working off-duty positions at grocery stores often ask about hidden rules regarding food. They say things like, "I don't care if someone is working for their money or receiving welfare, when it is payday I see folks in generational poverty come in and buy tons of groceries. Even things like steaks and shrimp. How is it that this same family has no food in the house when we visit them on a call two days later?"

Because life in poverty is about survival, you don't always know when you're going to be able to eat. So, one of the hidden rules about food in poverty is that when you have it, have a lot of it. You use food to celebrate, to make yourself feel better, and, of course, you share it with the people with whom you have relationships. If you ever go to a party in poverty, there will be more food than you know what to do with. It is expected that you will stuff yourself at this party *and* take a plate home. The question of concern is, "Did you get enough?" The point is that when you are fortunate enough to be able to eat, you eat a lot, and you worry about tomorrow when it comes.

People in middle class generally know that they are going to have food available later, so the question becomes, "Did the food taste good?" The emphasis is on the quality. People in middle class will eat for taste and for nutritional reasons. When officers are on a call in a middle class neighborhood, the cupboards often have food in them. Basic staples like sugar, rice, flour, seasonings, etc. are generally present. A hidden rule about food in middle class is that you keep the basics around because you want to be ready to cook the next meal.

POWER

In middle class, power and respect can be separated. A middle class worker might state, "I don't like my supervisor. Truth be told, I don't even respect my supervisor. But, my supervisor is the supervisor, and I respect the power that comes with that position; therefore, I follow my supervisor's instructions."

In poverty, power and respect are directly linked. If a worker in poverty does not respect a supervisor, then that worker may find it extremely difficult to take direction from that supervisor. In poverty, because your survival depends upon other people, it is hard to grant power to those for whom you have no respect. A badge or a title bestowed by an institution does not necessarily get one immediate respect from people in poverty. Relationships are the key to building respect in poverty, and that respect can be translated into power. Developing a relationship will enable an appropriate exchange of power and respect to take place; appealing to a title or to authority will not. This concept affects departments a great deal.

Recall this tool from Chapter 1:

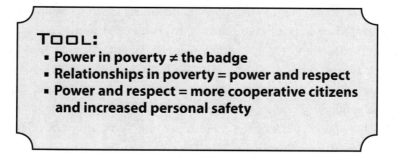

TOOL:
- **Power in poverty ≠ the badge**
- **Relationships in poverty = power and respect**
- **Power and respect = more cooperative citizens and increased personal safety**

In contrast, people in middle class are concerned with achievement and with sustaining their stabilized circle in the future. Others who hold titles and can affect one's achievement are often viewed as "powerful." They are not always respected, but others afford them the power that comes with their positions. Likewise, in wealth, it is necessary to maintain connections in order to sustain the circle and pass it on to future generations. Those who have the ability to change policy and direction are considered powerful, and people in wealth are taught to seek connections with them for this reason. Let's further investigate how this element can affect the careers of law enforcement personnel.

Middle class parents will often teach their young children to find a police officer if a strange person approaches them or if they become separated from their parents in public. The hidden rule in middle class is that police officers are helpful and good. People in middle class who have bad experiences with law enforcement officers usually head down to the department (which they still view as a good and powerful institution) and file a complaint, sure that the benevolent institution will reprimand its wayward employee.

As you may have experienced in your career, the attitude toward law enforcement in poverty can be much different. In fact, the police department often represents just one more institution that tells people in poverty what to do, and so the institution engenders little trust. Fortunately, relationships of mutual respect are powerful enough to override most of the suspicions someone may have about law enforcement. In a neighborhood in poverty you might hear something like, "Nope, even though Officer Jones is a cop, she's cool." This means that even though Officer Jones works for an institution that isn't highly trusted, she is viewed favorably because there is a relationship of mutual respect in place.

Police wield their power somewhat effortlessly in many middle class neighborhoods because of the status their position affords them in those communities. The power to arrest and jail citizens means that law enforcement personnel are in a position of authority that commands respect, and they are often treated with respect by people in middle class. In neighborhoods in poverty, and in those in wealth, your authority by itself can mean very little at times. Your standing within that community, meaning whether or not you are respected, will determine whether or not you are afforded power by the members of that community. The amount of power the members of a community afford you is directly related to the level of cooperation you will receive.

Please note that you feel respected when someone meets *your* expectations. Each officer has a personal set of expectations, and all of these sets of expectations vary. This means there are several different definitions of respect that a citizen has to figure out. For example: One officer may feel it is perfectly acceptable for a citizen to speak to police in what is perceived as a loud voice; however, another officer may find it disrespectful. The citizen is left constantly trying to understand what the officer presently handling the situation views as disrespectful.

TIME

In middle class, when your supervisor upsets you, what is your response? Is there a part of you that would like to tell your supervisor off? Why might a person in middle class choose not to tell a supervisor off?

In the heat of the moment, people in middle class might feel the urge to tell the supervisor off. However, people in middle class will quickly, almost unconsciously, start to process the moment in terms of the future, as in, "OK, if I give the supervisor a piece of my mind, then I could get fired, and then I would have to explain that to my partner/spouse. We wouldn't be able to afford our mortgage, I wouldn't have a good job reference, and then my career would … " In a split second the person in middle class processes the moment in terms of the future and, in most cases, chooses to remain quiet and let the supervisor finish, because doing anything else would be detrimental to the all-important future story.

After the incident, some will talk about the supervisor to co-workers, some will file an official grievance, and still others will go home and process it with a loved one. The point here is that people in middle class often perceive time in three distinct segments—past, present, and future—with the future being most important. People in middle class generally won't tell the boss off because of the future ramifications of doing so. The heat of the moment is often processed with the future in mind. How a given response will play out in the future is the primary mitigating factor for a person in middle class who must choose how to respond.

Many people in poverty work jobs that pay less than a livable wage. If you don't make enough money at your job to meet all your needs, it's relatively easy to get the same kind of job down the road, and you are not indebted to anyone for this particular job, what is your response likely to be when the supervisor does something to upset you? Many people in that situation will tell the supervisor off or simply quit. Why should you keep working a job for a person with whom you don't have a relationship and therefore don't respect when that job doesn't even meet your financial needs? In poverty time is perceived in terms of surviving the here and now. Often there is no grand future story to consider when choosing how to respond. There is a past to consider, but the past usually gets blended with the present moment. Law enforcement personnel have told me many stories in which they ask a witness in poverty about something that happened that day and the witness starts the response with a story about an event that happened three months previous. This demonstrates how the past can easily become wrapped up with the present moment.

The perception of time affects law enforcement a great deal. When law enforcement personnel spend the last three minutes at a scene trying to say something meaningful to the people involved so that law enforcement will not have to return, they often say things that are meaningful in terms of the future. For example, "Do this again and you are going to jail," or, "Now, we are clear: If I have to come back here, you will get a $50 ticket." A statement like this tends to be very meaningful to people in middle class because they will process it in terms of the future; the statements imply that the consequences will affect one's achievement, a meaningful thing for people in middle class. In poverty the criminal justice system is often perceived as an unavoidable, though unfortunate, part of your circle. Because people in poverty are focused on surviving today, rather than on the future, they are not worried by the threat of incarceration or a monetary fine, both of which are future events. The information is not processed in a way that makes it meaningful, and it will not garner a change in action.

> **TOOL:**
> **Translate the law into a meaningful form by basing your information on what the community perceives as meaningful.**

For example, restate the two statements above in ways that would be meaningful to people in poverty. It might go something like this: "So, we are clear that if you choose to have Billy monitor the music and keep it low, then you have chosen not to have to see my ugly mug again tonight?" Remember that humor is often appreciated in communities in poverty. You'll want to be sure to continue: "But, if you choose not to have Billy monitor the music, then you have chosen not only to see me again, but also to receive a fine. I know a fine might not be a big deal, but if you choose not to pay it, it turns into a warrant, and then three months from now, every time you see a squad car in the neighborhood, you'll be wondering if today's the day they called it in. It's your choice."

TALKING ABOUT CHANGE

Anyone can ask (or tell) another person to do something different—to change. That does not mean the other person will do it. It is only when something is said in a way that is meaningful that another person will respond in the desired manner. For example, you could tell me to lose weight all day long, but until the information is stated in a manner that is meaningful to me, there is a strong chance that I won't follow your advice. The analogy to law enforcement here should be pretty clear. Law enforcement personnel are constantly telling people to modify their behavior and/or actions so that law enforcement personnel will not have to return to the scene and take further action. Until law enforcement personnel are able to help people understand that what they are saying is meaningful, their advice falls on deaf ears.

Many law enforcement personnel will say, "But I *made* it meaningful: I told them that if they do it again, they'll go to jail." Refer back to the mental model of poverty. If you see jail as an unavoidable part of your circle, and you are focused solely on the here and now, then you don't perceive jail as a major threat. In middle class, however, because you don't want to be known as the person who went to jail last week, and because you immediately process the fact that being in jail will affect your future achievement, the same threat of incarceration is much more meaningful.

The point is that law enforcement workers should not focus solely on telling the truth; rather, they should focus on telling the truth *in an effective way*. If you told me today that I should lose weight, well, guess what? You're right. I am an intelligent person, and I am fully aware that carrying as much weight as I do on my frame can have some very serious health ramifications. Does that get me any closer to losing weight? No! A hundred people could tell me today that I should lose weight, and each one would be right. But I hope that being right, or that telling me the *truth* about my weight, keeps all one hundred people warm at night, because it certainly doesn't have the intended effect—i.e., getting me to lose weight. People may have all the information, but it is not until that information becomes meaningful to them that they will be motivated to change.

The ability to make things meaningful to others is what makes strong leaders effective. Perhaps you remember a time when the department made a personnel rule that got passed down to you without explanation and you were told to comply. You didn't understand why they changed the rule, no one asked for your input, and no one explained why this was happening. How did you or how would you feel in a situation like that? Many of us will grumble to each other about that rule, about the management, and about how they have nothing better to do with their time, right? Most people do not respond well to being told they must change. It is much easier to bring about effective, long-term change when individuals themselves identify the problems and suggest future solutions.

A research project published in the *Harvard Business Review* concluded that people in the criminal justice system cared as much about the *fairness* of the process through which an outcome was produced as they did about the outcome itself. The research project later defined *fairness* with three major principles: *Engagement* means involving individuals in the decisions that affect them by asking their input and allowing them to dispute the merits of another's ideas and assumptions. *Explanation* means that everyone who is involved in and affected by the decision should understand why final decisions are made as they are. Finally, an *expectation of clarity* requires that once a decision is made, the rules of the game are clearly stated. Law enforcement personnel generally practice these principles. Learning about hidden rules will assist with engagement and expectation setting, and learning how language functions in the three major economic classes will help with explanation.

Remember that almost every service organization is asking the citizen (client, customer, etc.) to change. Whether it is to eat healthier, smoke less, work more, get married, get divorced, be a more active parent, read to one's kids, keep one's music down, get this form to that place, stop fighting, whatever the organization's purpose is, ultimately the organization asks the person it serves to change so that the person receiving service won't need the service in the future. Change has a much better chance of happening when the person being asked to change processes the problem and helps determine what the solution will look like.

When I not only admit that I am overweight, but also admit that it is a problem and have enough space to process how it will look to lose the weight, *then* I stand a much better chance of making a long-term change. Ultimately, as an officer, do you want to drive home saying, "Well, I told them the truth"—or do you want to drive home saying, "Well, I was effective today"? To be effective doesn't mean that you don't tell the truth; it simply means that you tell the truth in a way that is meaningful and engages the people listening.

Now, if you're feeling like the approach outlined above is too "cute and sensitive" or "touchy-feely" to be effective, let's look at how it might work in an officer's own life: Think of a superior you did not like and didn't even respect. What was your response to this "bad leader?" Not working as hard, talking behind his/her back, showing less loyalty, and being generally uncooperative are just a few common responses. And when you had superiors you respected, even though you may not have agreed with them all the time, you had respect for them. What was your response to them? Cooperation, hard work, and loyalty are common. The minute you say you work in law enforcement, whether you are on the streets or answering the phones, you will be looked upon as a leader.

Whether you want to be a leader or not is somewhat irrelevant; officers are viewed as and are expected to be leaders in the community. If the communities you serve view you as a bad leader, then you should expect many of the responses listed above from the civilians you work with; they will be uncooperative and won't work as hard or give as much as they would if they viewed you as a good leader. One of the quickest ways to get labeled a bad leader is to say things in ways that are not meaningful to the people you are addressing. The tool above is about understanding the communities you work in, which will allow you to make your information meaningful, be viewed as a good leader, and thereby benefit from the positive responses good leaders generate.

FAMILY

Recall from the first chapter that people in middle class often have careers—not just a J-O-B—and that those careers give them an identity that is generally respected by the larger societal system. When one has access to a career, one has access to a different way of forming an identity. In their book *Promises I Can Keep,* Kathryn Edin and Maria Kefalas discuss how this element affects becoming a parent.

Do this exercise: Think of as many women as you can who are older than 23, single, have no children, and who live in middle class. Just think of as many as you can. Now think of as many women as you can who are older than 23, single, have no children, and live in poverty. Again, think of as many as you can. Many readers will be able to think of more women in middle class than in poverty. Why? One of several reasons is that women in middle class have access to many identities that society at large will acknowledge.

"What, young lady, you are going to be a *lawyer*?" When something like this is heard in middle class, it is often meant in a congratulatory manner, because the title "lawyer" gives one an identity that middle class acknowledges and honors. The young woman in question does not need to be, nor is she expected to have to be, a mother right now, which allows her to try to achieve a career-related identity. She has more than one way to achieve an identity that the societal system will honor. In poverty there is often less access to different kinds of respected identities; however, one identity that is still honored by society at large, and is still accessible, is "parent."

Statistics show us that single parenthood is more prominent in poverty than in other classes. In these cases the female is usually the primary parent; therefore, in poverty the matriarch generally has the primary relationship and thus holds much power within the family structure—even in the community at large.

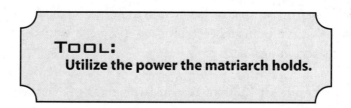

TOOL:
Utilize the power the matriarch holds.

In Chapter 1 we discussed a scenario in which it was the mother who ordered her son to go with an officer. When officers are called to a house to handle a domestic dispute in poverty, they will do well to look for the matriarch and speak with her. Often a man will step in and try to talk over her. At this point officers should move their attention to the man who interrupted. If another person involved in this call is on the scene, that person will jump in and interrupt him. There is no way this third person will let the officers talk only to *that guy*. Separate these two parties to keep yourself safe, and go back to the matriarch. I have seen matriarchs give a simple nonverbal that told others to step back. Building a relationship of mutual respect with the matriarch not only gives you power in your interactions with her, it also gives you power within the family structure and possibly within the community. Please note that the oldest woman on the scene is not necessarily the matriarch.

CONCLUSION

The communities that law enforcement personnel serve look and operate differently from one another. The hidden rules found in each community are different, and we must remember that it is not a matter of which set of hidden rules is "better" than others. No one can justify some of the things law enforcement officials see in wealth, middle class, and poverty. Again, the focus should not be on determining which system of hidden rules operates "better" than others; rather, care should be taken to learn to be effective with the people in each economic class you serve. Being effective means not only understanding the community and the people in it, but also developing the ability to translate the law in a way that is meaningful to each citizen. When citizens are able to recognize the significance of a law and how it will affect them personally, they are much more likely to obey it. Officers who are able to translate the law in meaningful ways are generally viewed as good leaders, which makes citizens more willing to cooperate with them and ultimately obey the law. When citizens obey the law, it not only proves law enforcement personnel effective, it also keeps them safe and makes the job easier.

Chapter Three

THE IMPORTANCE
OF LANGUAGE

Language is the primary mode of human communication, but not all people who speak the same language speak it in the same way. In a book called *The Five Clocks: A Linguistic Excursion into the Five Styles of English Usage,* Dutch linguist Martin Joos identified five different registers of language that range in usage from very intimate to very public. The register a person uses is often as strong a determinant of the outcome as the actual words being spoken. In fact, using the wrong register in a given situation can lead to misunderstandings, offense, and in some cases (like those involving intimate register used to sexually harass another person), disciplinary and/or legal action.

The following chart identifies each of the five registers and gives descriptions and examples:

REGISTERS OF LANGUAGE

REGISTER	EXPLANATION
FROZEN	Language that is always the same. For example: Lord's Prayer, wedding vows, etc.
FORMAL	The standard sentence syntax and word choice of work and school. Has complete sentences and specific word choice.
CONSULTATIVE	Formal register when used in conversation. Discourse pattern not quite as direct as formal register.
CASUAL	Language between friends and is characterized by a 400- to 800-word vocabulary. Word choice general and not specific. Conversation dependent upon nonverbal assists. Sentence syntax often incomplete.
INTIMATE	Language between lovers or twins. Language of sexual harassment.

Source: *Bridges Out of Poverty*, Payne, DeVol, Smith (2006)

Joos showed in his research that these five registers exist in every language. You will hear each register in every region. Different regions of the United States are often associated with particular registers, but these associations are popular misconceptions. All registers of language are found in all regions. For example, when people in the North hear a strong Southern drawl, they may assume the person is speaking in casual register. This assumption may be very inaccurate, as people with strong Southern accents can and do speak in the formal and frozen registers. Activities of the court, lectures at academic institutions, and corporate activities all take place in formal register in the South, and marriages, funerals, and church services are carried out using frozen register.

We see the opposite effect when people from the United States hear a strong British accent—they tend to think that the person is speaking in formal register. However, British people, like everyone else, utilize casual register too. All registers exist in all regions. How often a person speaks each register varies according to many factors, but to associate one register with a particular accent, region, or country is a false assumption that can easily cause a misunderstanding. And as law enforcement personnel well know, a simple misunderstanding has the potential to put an officer in danger very quickly.

People in generational middle class tend to use formal register more frequently than people in generational poverty. They use words to negotiate, revealing an important point about middle class: There is a strong emphasis on verbal communication and negotiation. People in generational poverty tend to use casual register more often than people in middle class and wealth. Language within casual register tends to be about survival—statements that get you through the moment. Linguistic research tells us that all humans rely on nonverbal signs when communicating; in casual register, the awareness of nonverbal signs is heightened.

NONVERBAL COMMUNICATION

In generational poverty, nonverbal communication (gestures, facial expressions, monosyllabic expressions, etc.) is emphasized. It is an external world; if you want to survive, you'd better feel it, hear it, or see it coming at you. Recall from Chapter 1 the house in generational poverty. There are often many people in one dwelling. When Uncle Fred comes home drunk, one needs to know if Uncle Fred is going to pass out or if he's going to start a fight. Uncle Fred never verbally articulates what he intends to do, but his nonverbals make it clear. Being able to see, feel, and hear nonverbal signals that are sent to you will help you survive in poverty; in fact, this ability is absolutely mandatory. Teachers have reported students in school hitting other students without recognizable provocation. When asked to explain the behavior, the aggressors' most common responses were along the lines of, "Because s/he was looking at me."

Absolutely! In poverty, if someone gives you a dangerous look, it may be in your best interest to attack preemptively before you yourself are attacked. Because nonverbal cues communicate information, they are being interpreted quickly and are relied upon as heavily as verbal communication. Law enforcement personnel must be conscious of what their nonverbals are communicating. I can't stress this enough: In a neighborhood in poverty, *nonverbal communication is as important as verbal communication.*

Consider this story once shared with me by a judge: The judge was having a difficult time with some of the people over whose cases he presided. More than one defendant had accused him of calling them stupid and being disrespectful toward them. This puzzled the judge because he had never called anyone in his courtroom "stupid," and he always tried hard to conduct himself in a respectful manner. When he asked his mentor about this, the mentor explained to him that his nonverbal gestures were sending that message. The defendants were most likely responding to the judge's negative nonverbal cues. Armed with the understanding that some people are more acutely aware of nonverbal communication than of the words being spoken, the judge returned to his court conscious of monitoring his nonverbals and experienced much greater success.

Developing an acute awareness of nonverbal communication will help law enforcement personnel on the job. In particular, developing an awareness of—and more importantly, the ability to control—one's own nonverbal cues will prove extremely useful. An easy test is to take a moment to focus on what that little voice in the back of your head is saying. It usually exerts unconscious control over your nonverbals. If you are approached by the same citizen with the same concern three times in one shift, and during these encounters that little voice in the back of your head is saying, "Wow, this person is *slow*," you will often reflect that sentiment unconsciously with your nonverbals. Though officers are trained to be professional and will address this person in a polite, professional manner, an officer's nonverbals may communicate very clearly what the officer is actually thinking. A person who lives in an environment in which knowing how to read nonverbals is a necessary survival skill will likely notice the message you're sending with your nonverbals. If the message is, "Wow, this person is *slow*," or something similar, one of two responses is likely: The person will either shut down or confront you and ask something like, "Why are you treating me this way?"

Another example: Record a new outgoing voicemail message on your phone, but first make yourself "tight" nonverbally. Cross your arms, lift your shoulders, make your facial expression blank, and then leave your voice message. Now listen to it. Next, record your message again, this time with open gestures, arms apart, a relaxed stance, and a smile on your face while you record your message. You will hear the difference in the messages. Our nonverbals can also affect the tone in which the message is delivered.

LANGUAGE FUNCTION: SURVIVAL AND NEGOTIATION

Within casual register, words are used to survive. When you live in an external world, commands like, "Sit down," "Stop it," "Start that," or, "Move it," are all the language of survival. They are words that will get you through this moment. They will help you survive. If children are to remain safe, they must follow directions. This is especially important in poverty. When someone yells out, "Get down!" you need to know your child will do so. In that situation, to have a child respond with words of negotiation—"Approximately how far down? And if I choose to get down, do I get a reward?"—will not aid survival; in fact, it can be detrimental. Words of survival ensure the safety of you and your loved ones and are expressed frequently within casual register.

In middle class words are used to negotiate. Words of negotiation are about bringing meaning to a situation in order to negotiate a behavior. For example, in middle class, parents might yell outside to their child, "Bobbie, come on in." But they know their Bobbie, and he is not coming in the first time he's called. So the middle class parents quickly bring meaning to the situation to negotiate the desired behavior. "Bobbie, come on in or your supper will get cold."

When Bobbie comes in and sits down at the table with filthy, dirty hands, his middle class parents will continue with words of negotiation. "Bobbie, didn't I see you playing under the old oak tree? Yes? Well, isn't that the oak tree that Mr. Johnson's dog always relieves himself on? Do you think your ma wants Mr. Johnson's dog's relief on her food? Please go wash your hands."

Formal register words of negotiation were being used with the child the entire time. This gives Bobbie access to the syntax and vocabulary of formal register; it also helps him assign meaning to the world around him. Because middle class is such a verbal world, people in middle class are eager to facilitate their children's verbal skills and thereby help the children understand the world around them. Highly developed verbal skills help children in middle class negotiate, stay safe, and achieve their goals.

Practicing negotiation using formal register teaches many cognitive lessons. Imagine you are a middle class parent who gets a phone call at 1 a.m. from the day care center stating they cannot watch your children today because a water pipe burst. At 1 a.m. there are only two people you can call: your mom and your sister. Your sister already has obligations and can't help you. Your mom agrees to watch the oldest two children, but not the youngest. Mom is getting older and cannot handle all three children. It becomes clear to you that you will have to take your 5-year-old daughter with you to the training you are going to attend for work that day.

As a middle class parent, what do you pack for her? Tons of quiet games, toys, and snacks. During the ride to the presentation site, you talk to the 5-year-old about what is coming up (future story) and what the expectations are (understanding the middle class rules in operation). Once you get to the site, you set up the quiet toys and games, set snacks out, and go through the expectations one more time. This time you inform your child that if she is loud, then the nice people around her will not be able to hear; but, if she is quiet, not only will people be able to hear, she will also get a yummy juice bottle at break time. If she starts to get louder, you will remind her that she is in jeopardy of losing the juice bottle.

What cognitive lessons did you nurture during this exchange? Most importantly you've reinforced the concepts of future orientation and sequence by constantly letting the child know what comes next and what the expectations will be. Choice is emphasized by letting the child know that if she chooses to remain quiet, she will get a reward, but if she chooses to be loud, she'll get nothing. Delayed gratification and consequence are also cognitive concepts being indirectly nurtured as a result of using formal language and words of negotiation.

In generational poverty you often wouldn't have time for all of that. In fact, the story might go something more like this: Your sister-in-law didn't show up to watch your children this morning, so you have to run through the neighborhood to find someone to watch them. While you are attempting to do this, the person who was going to give you a ride to work has to leave or she will be late for work. You finally get someone to agree to watch the two older children but not the youngest, so you take her with you. Because your ride left, you have to take the bus, which makes you nearly an hour late to your training site. When you come in the door, the entire audience is swearing at you— not verbally, but their nonverbals tell you very clearly that they are highly frustrated with you. You sit your daughter down and tell her, "Sit down and shut up," and then you pull out your tablet and pen and go to work. You only had time/need for words of survival, for language that would get you through the moment— a definite contrast with middle class and its emphasis on words of explanation and negotiation. A job in law enforcement requires one to understand both casual and formal register. While responsibilities like attending community meetings, courtroom appearances, and meetings with supervisors call for formal register and words of negotiation, such duties as directing citizens while on an active crime scene often call for survival-oriented words in casual register. Understanding the different registers and how the different economic groups utilize them gives you more insight into how and why people respond to you in the register of language that they do.

DISCOURSE PATTERNS AND STORY STRUCTURE

The differences between casual and formal register mentioned above—vocabulary, words of negotiation versus words of survival, and verbal communication versus nonverbal communication—are not the only differences. The discourse patterns also vary. Recall the citizen who was asked about something that happened that day and whose answer started with something that happened three months ago. As you tried to follow this long story of what happened, you probably found it hard to keep track because so many people and so many seemingly unrelated events were mentioned. This is because the two different registers use two different discourse patterns. In formal register the discourse pattern is direct, while in casual register it is circular. People in middle class use formal register often; therefore, they generally tell a story in a very direct way, starting with the first event and recounting the rest of the events that led to the most recent event. Usually the story builds up to the most important points and then comes down with a concluding sentence or two. In contrast, people in generational poverty tend to use casual register, and the casual register story is told in a circular pattern.

Kaplan Discourse

Formal Register Discourse Pattern

Casual Register Discourse Pattern

Speaker gets straight to the point.

Speaker goes around the issue before finally coming to the point.

Source: *Bridges Out of Poverty,* Payne, DeVol, Smith (2006)

Story Structure

Formal Register Story Structure

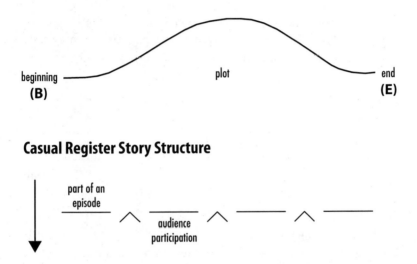

Source: *Bridges Out of Poverty,* Payne, DeVol, Smith (2006)

The graphics above provide mental models of the two different story structures. The formal register story has a clear beginning (B), and the action builds up to the main plot element or the point of the story. Then the action tapers back down to a clear ending (E). Remember this hidden rule about time in middle class: It is viewed in terms of the past, present, and future. For this reason the story moves chronologically. The point of the story is to share information, so it is designed to cover the necessary elements from the past, make a point regarding the present and/or the future, and let everybody move on. Have you ever been in a middle class community meeting where someone simply fails to make a point and move on? Painful, isn't it? To people who are used to hearing and telling stories that are presented in a clear-cut, chronological structure, a circular story structure does not seem to meet the goal of information sharing.

In generational poverty, because the casual story structure is used, there is no straightforward beginning. A person may start a story by relating something that occurred three months ago, or start with an entirely different story he or she feels is necessary background information—e.g., "I told you that story to tell you this one … "

As the story progresses, there are points at which audience participation is acceptable. At times it is even expected. The small insertion markers in the mental model represent places in the story where, if there is a relationship with the listeners, the listeners are expected to jump in with commentary or share experiences of their own. This casual register story structure is as much about being entertaining as it is about sharing information.

If a person in poverty is telling a law enforcement worker a story, and the person is thinking that the law enforcement worker is "OK" but for some reason is not participating in the storytelling, the person may give verbal cues or make gestures that indicate the law enforcement worker should jump in. Such statements as, "You know what I mean?" and, "You get what I'm sayin'?" may be used to encourage a listener to join in. After an appropriate interjection from a listener, the story continues until the next opportune place for audience participation. Often there is no clear ending to the story. Sometimes a listener may take the story in a completely different direction, and sometimes the person telling the story just stops it. The story itself will tend not to move chronologically. The past may be in the middle, the present at the end, and the beginning was "another story I had to tell you before I could get to this one."

CASE STUDY: WALTER (CAUCASIAN MALE)

The following story from *Bridges Out of Poverty* is based on an actual court case heard in Houston, Texas during March 1995. The bold print indicates the "narrator's" story that came out in the trial; the plain print indicates the kinds of comments that might be made by others if this was a story being told in generational poverty by a relative or neighbor.

Well, you know Walter got put away for 37 years. Him being 48 and all. He'll probably die in jail. Just couldn't leave his hands off that 12-year-old Susie.

Dirty old man. Bodding's gonna whup his tail.

Already did. You know Bodding was waiting for him in jail and beat the living daylights out of him.

In jail?

Yeah, Bodding got caught for possession. Had $12,000 on him when they arrested him.

Golly, wish I had been there to cash in!!!! (laughter) A man's gotta make a living!

Susie being blind and all—I can see why Bodding beat the daylights out of Walter. Lucky he didn't get killed, old Walter is.

Too bad her momma is no good.

She started the whole thing! Susie's momma goes over there and argues with Bodding.

Ain't they divorced?

Yeah, and she's got Walter working for her, repairing her house or something.

Or something, I bet. What's she got in her house that's worth fixing?

Anyway, she goes over to Bodding's house to take the lawnmower . . .

I reckon so as Walter can mow the yard?? I bet that's the first time old Walter has ever broken a sweat! Reminds me of the time I saw Walter thinking about taking a job. All that thinking and he had to get drunk. He went to jail that time, too—a felony, I think it was. So many of those DWIs. Judge told him he was egregious. Walter said he wasn't greasy—he took a bath last week!!! (laughter)

Bodding and Susie's momma got in a fight, so she tells Walter to take Susie with him.

Lordy, her elevator must not go all the way to the top!! Didn't she know about him getting arrested for enticing a minor???

With Susie blind and all. And she sends Susie with Walter?

She sure don't care about her babies.

Well, Walter's momma was there 'cause Walter lives with his momma, seeing as how he can't keep no job.

Ain't his other brother there?

Yeah, and him 41 years old. That poor momma sure has her burdens to bear. And then her 30-year-old daughter, Susie's momma, at home, too. You know Susie's momma lost custody of her kids. Walter gets these videos, you know. Those adult videos. Heavy breathing! (laughter)

Some of them are more fun to listen to than look at! (laughter) Those people in the videos are des-per-ate!!

Anyway, he puts those on and then carries Susie to his room and tells her she wants him—and describes all his sex-u-al exploits!!

Golly, he must be a loooooooooover. (laughter) He should be shot. I'd kill him if he did that to my kid!!

Then he lets his fingers do the walking.

Kinda like the Yellow Pages! (laughter)

I guess he didn't do anything with his "thang," according to Miss Rosie who went to that trial every day. And Susie begging him to stop so many times.

Probably couldn't do anything with it; that's why he needs to listen to that heavy breathing! Pant! Pant! (laughter) What a no-count, low-down creep. I'll pay Bodding to kill him!!

Bodding says the only way Walter is coming out of jail is in a pine box.

Don't blame him myself.

Yeah, Miss Rosie said Walter's momma said at the trial that the door to Walter's room was open and there ain't no way Walter could have done that. That she is a good Christian momma and she don't put up with that.

Oh Lordy, did God strike her dead on the spot, or is she still alive??? I'd be afraid of ending up in eternal damnation for telling a story like that!

Miss Rosie said her 12-year-old nephew testified that the door was closed and his grandma told him to say it was open!!!!

Ooo! Ooo! Oooo! That poor baby tells the truth? His grandma's gonna make him mis-er-a-ble!!!

And then Walter's momma tells that jury that she never allows those adult videos in her house, leastways not that she pays for them!! (lots of laughter)

I bet the judge bit on that one!! How is Walter gonna get videos except for her money? Mowing yards? (more laughter) No, I bet he saves his pennies!! (laughter)

All these years she has covered for Walter. Guess she just couldn't cover no more.

Remember that time Walter got drunk and wrecked her car, and she said she was driving? And she was at the hospital at the time with a broken leg. And the judge asked her how she could be driving and in the hospital "simultaneously." And she said that's just how it was—simultaneously—she had never felt so excited in her life. (laughter) Who turned Walter in?

Well, it wasn't Susie's momma. She was busy with Skeeter, her new boyfriend. I hear he's something.

Remember that one boyfriend she had? Thought he was so smart?

Speaking of smart, that Susie sure is. Her blind and all, and she won the district spelling bee for the seventh grade this year. I hear she's in National Honor Society, whatever that is.

Wonder if it's kinda like the country club. Instead of playing golf, you just spell!!! (laughter)

Susie calls this friend of hers who tells her mother and they come and get her and take her to the police and hospital.

Some rich lady, not minding her own business, that's for sure.

Well, it was a good thing for Susie, 'cause that momma of hers sure ain't good for Susie. She don't deserve a kid like Susie. SHE oughta be the one who's blind.

Ain't that the truth. Way I see it, she already is. Just look at Skeeter!! (gales of laughter)

If law enforcement personnel hear a story like this and get frustrated, their nonverbals will communicate that frustration—unless they have learned to control them. If you work in law enforcement and give off even just a few negative nonverbals, your witness will either shut down on you or confront you. In the case that the witness confronts you, the scenario often plays out something like this: The witness says, "So you think you're mister big guy just 'cause you got a badge and a gun? I don't need this crap! I got things at home I need to take care of," and starts to walk away. You call the witness back, but also recall the hidden rules: Because there is no relationship in place, this witness may not come back. This lack of feeling beholden may be expressed verbally, as in, "You don't mean nothin' to me!" So the person keeps walking. If your next move is to immobilize the person on the hood of your squad car and make an arrest for either obstructing the investigation or fleeing, you may find that the person is still "mouthing off" to you as you make the arrest. "Oh, you think you're real big now just 'cause you got a badge, a gun, and handcuffs. Yeah, you're a real big man now. Just for the record, I've had the handcuffs on tighter!"

When people in this situation get to jail, they feel they have been completely and totally wronged. In addition, law enforcement personnel feel more frustration with the population than ever before—all because of a huge but generally unrecognized miscommunication.

TOOL:

When you encounter a circular story spoken in causal register, do three things:

First, listen to the story to gather a clear idea of the information. Enjoy the story—it is meant to be entertaining, and it usually is. Note that many times the story will also include useful information for you regarding other things in the neighborhood. Though I may be answering your questions about the description of the person who robbed the corner store, I might also say, "Well, Jackie—y'know, the girl selling outta her car over on 42nd—well, she's been seeing the guy who robbed the store, and I don't like her at all." Did you need to know that I don't like Jackie? No, but knowing that she's dating the suspect may be useful later. Numerous small pieces of information flow out of a story when witnesses feel comfortable talking. Listen for those pieces of information. Let things you *don't* need to hear about roll past you; however, if a potentially important point is unclear, jump in: "Your old man's cousin? Now how does he fit into all of this again?"

Sometimes you will not have time to hear a long, circular story. In these cases you may need to interrupt someone, but the interruption will be better received if you say something like this: "This sounds like a great story, and I appreciate you telling me, but in order for me to help your community (or your friend), I'm gonna need to cut you off and ask you exactly what he looks

(continued on next page)

25

(continued from previous page)

like. Once I have that description and I can get the rest of the department looking for this guy, then I can listen to the rest of the story. OK? So tell me exactly what color cap did he have on?" The point here is to honor the fact that someone is talking to you, state that you're interrupting in order to help the community or someone with whom the person has a relationship, and show that you will let the person tell the story in the future. Be sure to return and listen to the story so that you can collect those small pieces of information discussed above.

Second, always watch your nonverbals. If you need information for an arrest, you need to be conscious of the message your nonverbals are sending. Negative nonverbals will lead to a witness shutting down or confronting you. Either response makes law enforcement personnel less successful at retrieving useful information.

Finally, after the witness is done telling you the information, tell it back to the witness in formal register as a way to clarify. Take it slow. If it was hard for you to understand the story in casual register, it is equally hard for some people to follow the story in formal register. However, retelling the story in formal register ensures that you've collected accurate information.

FUTURE ORIENTATION, CHOICE, AND POWER

If an individual depends upon a random, episodic story structure for memory patterns, lives in an unpredictable environment, and has not developed the ability to plan, THEN …

If an individual cannot plan, he/she **cannot predict.**

If an individual cannot predict, he/she **cannot identify cause and effect.**

If an individual cannot identify cause and effect, he/she **cannot identify consequence.**

If an individual cannot identify consequence, he/she **cannot control impulsivity.**

If an individual cannot control impulsivity, he/she **has an inclination toward criminal behavior.**

Adapted from the work of Reuven Feuerstein

Source: *Bridges Out of Poverty,* Payne, DeVol, Smith (2006)

When no one intervenes, law enforcement personnel see the scenario described above play out in a short period of time. Let's examine it point by point.

If an individual depends upon a random, episodic story structure for memory patterns ... The story structure with which we're most comfortable also affects our patterns of memory. An individual whose memories are primarily stored according to the casual register story structure retains information in a sporadic, circular manner. But most law enforcement personnel ask for information in a linear, chronological form. This has an impact on a department's effectiveness in interviewing.

... lives in an unpredictable environment ... The mental model of poverty demonstrated that many citizens from poverty do not have the privilege of living in a stable environment.

... does not have the ability to plan ... Officers often witness this element. I frequently hear officers say things like, "Jodi, he knew step one, but two and three seemed to elude him."

... cannot predict ... This means that the person is not taking the information or moment at hand and thinking about how it will play out in the future. This occurs when one is concerned about surviving and less invested in a future scenario.

... cannot identify consequence ... Think about the witness from poverty who walked away from an officer even as the officer told her to come back. That woman probably wasn't thinking, "Oh, wait a minute, if I don't listen to the officer, then he can arrest me, which means I spend at least two days in jail until I am arraigned and out. That would be two days everyone would be at my apartment without me, and I am supposed to work tomorrow." If one does not process each step above, then you can begin to see how that person may not see consequences coming.

Officers have seen this process played out by citizens they work with. While it is helpful to understand the cycle, the tools below can actually prevent it from occurring.

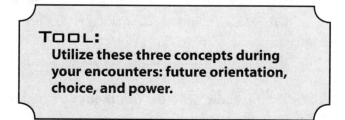

TOOL:
Utilize these three concepts during your encounters: future orientation, choice, and power.

In the sequence outlined on the previous page, people may not see the consequences coming (future orientation), may feel that there is no choice in the matter, and/or may feel like there is no opportunity to voice objections; consequently, people in this situation can feel like things just happen to them (no feeling of power).

Future orientation, choice, and power are three concepts that offer people ways to reframe their encounters with law enforcement and can stop the cycle outlined above from occurring. If one is processing this moment in terms of the future, one tends to see consequences; if one feels one has power and knows the choices available, then one can choose other actions and avoid going through each step of the cycle outlined above. Sharing these three concepts with the people you encounter ensures that they see what is coming and feel they have choice and power in the situation. The next tool is a practical way to utilize this.

> **TOOL:**
> **"If you choose, then you have chosen," is a sentence that enhances the concepts in the last tool: future orientation, choice, and power.**

A sentence I must use 50 times a day when I'm in the field is, "If you choose X, then you've chosen Y." This simple sentence enhances all three concepts—future orientation, choice, and power. Let's break this down point by point as well.

If you ... This means that the individual is in control and has power.

... choose ... This teaches that there are choices.

... then ... This strengthens the concept of cause and effect.

... you've chosen ... This builds future orientation and awareness of consequences.

Though this sentence nurtures all three crucial concepts, it must always be used twice to illustrate at least two options. Saying only, "If you choose to keep your music up loud, then you've chosen a fine," doesn't do a sufficient job of presenting the concept of power through choice. Use the sentence structure twice. Say, "Or, if you choose to turn it down so your neighbors quit calling, you've chosen not to see me again today and to spend that $200 on something cool instead of on a public nuisance ticket." Be a fork in the road so that citizens on the verge of making harmful or costly decisions can pause and reconsider. It can be hard not to take some behaviors personally, but one has to remember that one doesn't know what a given citizen has been through that day. Some have been battered, some haven't eaten, some are unsure where they will live next week. Present a civilian with the opportunity to consider: You choose this behavior, and here is what you have chosen; you choose this other behavior, and you've chosen something entirely different.

REFRAMING: MAKING INFORMATION MEANINGFUL BY TAPPING INTO CITIZENS' MOTIVATION

It is vital that whatever you say after " ... then you have chosen ... " be meaningful to the citizen, but please note that it doesn't necessarily have to be meaningful to you. For example, let's say you work for a police department and you have a domestic call in a middle class neighborhood involving a man who is alleged to have assaulted his wife. When you arrive on the scene, you separate everyone, ensure that the scene is safe, and start talking to the victim. As you speak to her, her husband starts to get upset. You turn to him and say, "Hey, settle down or I will have to take you to jail." This is a very meaningful statement to most middle class men because their thinking is future-oriented. The badge represents power in their community, and the instability caused by going to jail can threaten their achievement. The middle class husband sees immediately that getting arrested in front of the neighbors will not be good for his or his family's reputation, not to mention the fact that his wife will have to bail him out, a burden both financial and emotional. The future ramifications start to outweigh the current situation.

People in middle class also see information and institutions as ways to maintain some power in a situation, so the man might say, "Fine, I'll settle down. I would like your name and badge number. I will take this up with your superiors." The middle class man can maintain some power and control in the moment by gathering information he can use later to file a complaint with the police department, the institution that wields power over citizens and individual officers. The point is that the information you presented was meaningful to the recipient, and the recipient demonstrated knowledge of the three concepts by taking what you said, thinking about how it would play out in the future, seeing a choice, and finding a way to maintain power in the situation. Therefore, the statement you made to him as an officer was ultimately effective.

Now let's imagine the same scene as it might transpire in poverty. Same domestic call, you have everyone separated, you are talking to the victim, and the man starts to get upset. If you say the same sentence in poverty that you used in middle class, "Hey, settle down or I will have to take you to jail," it tends not to have the same effect because it isn't nearly as meaningful to the person in poverty. He is focused on the right now, and your badge alone is not enough to convince him of your power and authority. It is not that this man is not motivated—he is—but the concerns that motivate him are very different than the concerns that motivate the man in middle class. Say something like this: "Hey, Fred is it? I see what you're sayin'. I patrol this area, and I've seen Bob hanging out over here. I've never seen *your* lady talk to him, but I see him in this area. All I am sayin' is that if you don't settle down and work with me, you know I gotta take you in. What is it, about two days in jail before they let you out and you can get back here? That's two days Bob would be running around the neighborhood free while you're locked up." Even though Fred may not want to work with law enforcement, he wants even less to leave Bob alone in the community, especially around his family and his partner. Now you have reframed your information in a way that makes it meaningful to Fred and enhances the concepts of future orientation, choice, and power. The more officers understand the communities they police, the more they can translate the law in ways that are meaningful enough to tap into anyone's motivation; this keeps officers safer and makes the job easier.

The problem is not that citizens are not motivated; the problem is that we often fail to make our information appeal to the factors that motivate each citizen. This is one of the main challenges facing people who choose law enforcement as a career. Law enforcement personnel do not get to choose their clients. They must police the poorest of the poor and wealthiest of the wealthy—*and* they must hold them all accountable to the same laws.

ACCOUNTABILITY

Accountability is a key concept, and I make a point to emphasize its importance in my trainings. It is almost impossible to create a relationship of mutual respect with people if you do not hold each other accountable within the relationship. It is because I love and respect my family that I am also going to be honest with them, hold them accountable to a certain standard, and expect them to do the same for me. In this way, holding people accountable can be a form of respect. Law enforcement officers have a clear standard to uphold—the law—which cannot be lowered. Still, if law enforcement officers try to meet that standard by using the hidden rules from their own communities, rather than the hidden rules of the community they are working in, those officers will find themselves stressed out and increasingly ineffective. The same will happen if officers assume that people have resources they do not, or if they communicate using only one register and one story structure. Those officers also run the risk of seeming hypocritical if they are acting in this manner and at the same time demanding accountability. Accountability keeps our society safe and so must be demanded from every citizen. But the way in which that accountability is demanded is a key determinant of one's justness and fairness. The more tools officers have that work for each particular community, the more meaningful they'll be able to make the information, the better they can stay in control, and the safer and easier their jobs will be.

VOICES

Most people have all three voices and have used them before. The child voice is the one we turn to when we want to "whine" about the supervisor, as in, "The supervisor likes you more than me! You got your vacation request approved and I didn't!"

The parent voice is the one we turn to when we want to take control. If a fire broke out, I would use my parent voice to take control. "You, get out over there! You, go to the right!"

THREE VOICES

Adapted from the
work of Eric Berne

THE CHILD VOICE *
Defensive, victimized, emotional, whining, losing
attitude, strongly negative nonverbal.

- Quit picking on me.
- You don't love me.
- You want me to leave.
- Nobody likes (loves) me.
- I hate you.
- You're ugly.
- You make me sick.
- It's your fault.
- Don't blame me.
- She, he, _____ did it.
- You make me mad.
- You made me do it.

* *The child voice is also playful, spontaneous, curious,
etc. The phrases listed often occur in conflictual or
manipulative situations and impede resolution.*

THE PARENT VOICE * **
Authoritative, directive, judgmental, evaluative, win-lose mentality, demanding, punitive, sometimes threatening.

- You shouldn't (should) do that.

- It's wrong (right) to do _____ .

- That's stupid, immature, out of line, ridiculous.

- Life's not fair. Get busy.

- You are good, bad, worthless, beautiful (any judgmental, evaluative comment).

- You do as I say.

- If you weren't so _____ , this wouldn't happen to you.

- Why can't you be like _____ ?

* *The parent voice can also be very loving and supportive. The phrases listed usually occur during conflict and impede resolution.*

** *The internal parent voice can create shame and guilt.*

THE ADULT VOICE
Nonjudgmental, free of negative nonverbal, factual, often in question format, attitude of win-win.

- In what ways could this be resolved?

- What factors will be used to determine the effectiveness, quality of _____ ?

- I would like to recommend _____ .

- What are choices in this situation?

- I am comfortable (uncomfortable) with _____ .

- Options that could be considered are _____ .

- For me to be comfortable, I need the following things to occur: _____ .

- These are the consequences of that choice/action: _____ .

- We agree to disagree.

Source: *Bridges Out of Poverty*, Payne, DeVol, Smith (2006)

In contrast, if I was teaching a group of people how to evacuate a room in case of a fire, I would use the adult voice. Teaching occurs in the adult voice. When law enforcement workers need to take control of a situation, they will often use the parent voice. However, in the last three minutes on a call, when they are trying to say something that will prevent them from having to come back, they will want to use the adult voice, which is the best voice for fostering learning. If they use the parent voice to try to teach the concepts when there is no immediate threat, people may feel that they are being patronized and/or bossed around and will not respond well.

> ## TOOL:
> **Many children in poverty possess and use the parent voice.**

Due to the instability that is caused by trying to survive in poverty, some older children must care for their younger siblings. Thus some children learn to use the parent voice out of necessity. Children in this situation are very likely to respond negatively if a law enforcement worker with whom they don't have a relationship speaks to them in the parent voice. In the child's view, the child is the one who uses that voice (the parent voice)—not the police. Couple this with the fact that the child is more invested in this moment than in the future and it becomes easy to understand why the child gets upset with the law enforcement worker.

Children in middle class, on the other hand, often respond to the parent voice by backing off. This is because power in middle class is often associated with position, and because there is an emphasis on future stories and ramifications. The child associates the uniform and the badge with a position of power, hears a voice of authority from that person of power, sees the ramifications of noncompliance, and generally complies. The tools within this book are meant to be used after a scene or situation is under control; therefore, all the tools should be conducted in the adult voice.

CONCLUSION

The register of language to which people were exposed most while growing up affects their communication patterns. Law enforcement workers quickly learn that not all citizens communicate in the same register or with the same story structure. While some communities emphasize nonverbal communication, other communities rely heavily on verbal communication. While some will use words for negotiation, others will use words of survival. Likewise, the three voices every person has—parent, child, and adult—will get different responses in different situations and communities. As law enforcement personnel master the information in the language section and understand how it affects the people they serve and protect, they will find that getting information from witnesses becomes easier, their questioning of suspects becomes more powerful, and they are better able to hold people accountable. The bottom line is that law enforcement personnel can make tactical use of this information regarding communication just as they would be tactical in monitoring a protest or raiding a known drug house.

When utilized to its fullest, tactical communication will increase an officer's effectiveness and safety within all three economic communities.

Chapter Four

RESOURCES

> **CRISIS** = When an individual has few or no resources to draw upon in a given situation.

The table on the following page lists the eight resources originally identified by Ruby Payne in *A Framework for Understanding Poverty*. It also includes three additional resources identified by Philip DeVol in collaboration with people from poverty during the development of *Getting Ahead in a Just-Gettin'-By World*. The table reproduced here is from *Getting Ahead*.

DEFINITION OF RESOURCES

FINANCIAL
Having the money to purchase goods and services.

EMOTIONAL
Being able to choose and control emotional responses, particularly to negative situations, without engaging in self-destructive behavior. This is an internal resource and shows itself through stamina, perseverance, and choices.

MENTAL
Having the mental abilities and acquired skills (reading, writing, computing) to deal with daily life.

SPIRITUAL
Believing in divine purpose and guidance.

PHYSICAL
Having physical health and mobility.

SUPPORT SYSTEMS
Having friends, family, and backup resources available to access in times of need. These are external resources.

RELATIONSHIPS/ROLE MODELS
Having frequent access to adult(s) who are appropriate, who are nurturing to the child, and who do not engage in self-destructive behavior.

KNOWLEDGE OF HIDDEN RULES
Knowing the unspoken cues and habits of a group.

INTEGRITY AND TRUST
Trust is linked to two issues: predictability and safety. Can I know with some certainty that this person will do what he/she says? Can I predict with some accuracy that it will occur every time? The second part of the question is safety: Will I be safe with this person?

MOTIVATION AND PERSISTENCE
Having the energy and drive to prepare for, plan, and complete projects, jobs, and personal changes.

FORMAL REGISTER
Having the vocabulary, language ability, and negotiation skills to succeed in work and/or school environments.

Source: *Getting Ahead in a Just-Gettin'-By World,* Philip E. DeVol (2006)

MORE THAN JUST MONEY

Resources affect the stability individuals, institutions, and communities will be able to demonstrate and maintain. In the United States we have often looked at poverty as a one-resource issue, by which I mean we examine the financial aspect of poverty and call the case closed. However, there are many resources in play. In fact, the graphic on the previous page identifies 11 resources that are directly related to the issue. Please note that people in poverty analyzed this information and contributed the last three resources because they felt these were so essential they needed to be included.

Officers have spoken about coming into contact with citizens who have an abundance of financial resources (a person could have $20 million to her name), but because their other ten resources are underdeveloped, they have a difficult time maintaining stable circles. On the other hand, law enforcement workers have met families who are struggling economically, yet they are rich in the other ten resources. Those families often are able to maintain a higher level of stability in their circles and lives than are others in their neighborhoods. Due to their high level of resources, they have something to draw upon when they encounter a stressful situation. Having resources prevents the situation from escalating into a crisis. This means the police usually are not called. Officers generally find themselves being called during times of crisis, when resources are exhausted or unavailable. The more resources people and communities can demonstrate, the less frequently police intervention is needed.

> **TOOL:**
> Know which resources are available in a community and which institutions help people build resources. Connect the civilian with the proper institution. The more resources people have access to, the more stability they are able to maintain, which results in fewer calls to law enforcement to resolve issues.

Officers will want to become aware of the resources an individual has and the resources available in the community. Knowing which resources are available and how to access them can be very beneficial on the job. While officers do not have time to be social workers, they can often see that an individual could use assistance with a resource and can connect that individual with the person or agency that can help. If an individual does not get access to those who can assist with building a resource, this may result in further instability in that person's circle. This then increases the chances that law enforcement will be called upon again to deal with the same individual.

Take for example an officer who keeps getting calls to an apartment in Section 8 housing. The mother and daughter in the apartment are always fighting. As the officer drives up to the apartment building for yet another call, he can hear the two yelling at each other from the parking lot. After separating the mother and daughter, he asks them what is going on and explains that he has been there too many times for this to be a misunderstanding. The mother states that her daughter was not listening and was not acting herself. The officer knows of a mental health counseling service in the community, so he has the mother place a call and set up an appointment for her and her daughter. The next time he sees them in the neighborhood, he asks them how they are doing. Both report that they are doing much better and have not had law enforcement come to the apartment since they saw him last.

This story serves as an example of an officer making an appropriate and useful recommendation because he is aware of the resources available in the community in which he works. He has also reduced the likelihood that more valuable law enforcement time will be spent resolving the issue. More importantly, he has left these citizens with a favorable view of law enforcement personnel; this viewpoint will benefit all other law enforcement officers who may interact with these citizens in the future.

TALKING WITH PEOPLE ABOUT THEIR RESOURCES

When talking to individuals about their resources, it's best not to address deficits directly. No one responds well to this: "Hey, you're fat. Your physical resources are low. That's dangerous for your health. You need to lose weight." Rarely will this kind of "help" motivate a person to develop a resource or change a behavior. A better strategy is to address a resource that the person has a lot of before you contrast it with areas where resources are low.

A team of nurses working in a neighborhood in poverty was very frustrated that no one in the neighborhood would work to control a disease that was affecting many of them—diabetes. The nurses kept telling the adults from the community that if they did not take medicine and make appropriate lifestyle changes, they would die. But when you live in poverty and your world is about the here and now, there are other, more pressing things that could kill you sooner.

What the nurses were saying was true; however, the way in which they were presenting the information to their clients was not having the desired effect. When asked what resources their customers had a lot of, the nurses responded by saying that their relationships were very strong. With this in mind, they tried a new tack. Rather than telling their customers they were in danger of dying, the nurses asked them who would care for their grandchildren if they were not around, since many of the people at risk were raising their absent children's children. Showing them the importance of being there for their grandchildren was enough to motivate the customers to take their insulin and re-evaluate their choices regarding diet, exercise, etc.

Communities and individuals are influenced by the resources available to them. When one grows up in a family or community where there is no access to jobs that pay a livable wage, reliable transportation, or relationships that nurture emotional resources and a sense of integrity, it will affect one's experience and, hence, one's behavior. When we view people in terms of the resources that they hold and the resources available in their communities, we will begin to understand how and why behaviors and experiences are different. For example, after coming off the third call in a year to a very wealthy house, an officer stated, "I just don't get how someone with that much money can act this way and always be in crisis."

> **TOOL:**
> Use a resource the civilian has a lot of in order to address resources that are not present. Many times in law enforcement the truth may be on the law enforcement worker's side, but that doesn't make the truth effective unless law enforcement can enable citizens to view it in a way that makes it meaningful.

If we view stability as only being affected by one resource, money, then it's true that the behavior demonstrated is baffling. However, when we view the situation in terms of all the resources (especially emotional resources and integrity), we note that the people on the scene are visibly low in many areas; now we can begin to understand the resulting behavior. As stated earlier, understanding does not mean an officer lowers the expectations for people, but the ability to understand the behaviors being presented makes the behaviors easier to work with and prevent in the future.

When law enforcement personnel see the people they serve in terms of the resources they possess, then the law enforcement officers can better understand why people are responding in one manner or another. This understanding can make the job easier and thereby reduce job-related stress, provide law enforcement workers with more choice in their responses, and ultimately keep them safer.

If law enforcement personnel view all individuals and communities in terms of the resources to which they themselves have access, rather than the ones that are actually available, it will be frustrating because they will not see the behavior they expect to see. This can cause law enforcement personnel a lot of stress, and in some cases leads them to make reactionary judgments that cause loss of control of a situation—a very dangerous place to be.

CONCLUSION

The amount of resources one has access to and can demonstrate directly affects the stability of that person's circle (or life). When people have limited resources to draw upon, this puts them in the position of being repeatedly in crisis. Law enforcement personnel are called when there is a crisis. To reduce the frequency of crisis calls, one should address the resource issue.

Identify which resources civilians have a lot of, and use those resources to make your information "click" with them—to make it meaningful to them. The more meaningful it is to them, the better the chance they have of increasing their resources. Every community will look different based on the resources present. Law enforcement personnel can benefit greatly by knowing the resources available within the particular communities in which they work. Law enforcement personnel are not social service workers, nor should they be, but the ability to link citizens up with the agencies that can help them build resources (and thereby enhance the stability of their circles) can prevent law enforcement from being called back repeatedly to assist the same people.

It also helps a great deal for law enforcement personnel to be aware of the resources they personally grew up with and to keep in mind that not all the citizens with whom they come in contact will have had the same access to resources. The goal should be to observe the resources citizens demonstrate, connect them to resources within the community when possible, make your information more meaningful by highlighting the resources civilians are rich in, understand where they are coming from without condoning unacceptable or illegal behavior, and to thereby serve and protect as effectively as possible.

Law enforcement personnel can continue to be heroes day in and day out, but if resources continue to decline in a community, the job will be more difficult and busier than ever. In order to see a sustained, dramatic reduction in crime, resources in the community and within individuals have to be increased. If social services, educators, politicians, and community members (to name a few) do not work toward effectively building the resources in a community, officers will continue to face a difficult job.

Chapter Five

USING THIS INFORMATION
THROUGHOUT YOUR CAREER

In an appendix to *Bridges Out of Poverty: Strategies for Professionals and Communities* titled "Additive Model: aha! Process's Approach to Building Sustainable Communities," Phil DeVol outlined four areas of research on the causes of poverty that exist on a continuum ranging from the micro—individual choices and behaviors—to the macro—political and economic structures. These areas of research and their impact and assumptions were later discussed in more detail in the workbook designed to accompany *Bridges Out of Poverty.* As you advance in your career in law enforcement, the job will demand that you broaden your focus from the micro to the macro and begin to address systemic issues that allow or even perpetuate the kinds of situations officers are called to deal with every day. Let's look now at the poverty research continuum:

Poverty Research Continuum

CAUSES	Behaviors of the Individual	Absence of Human and Social Capital	Human Exploitation	Political/ Economic Structures
RESEARCH TOPICS	Dependence on welfare Behavior of individuals Individual morality Behaviors of groups Single parenthood Intergenerational character traits Poor parenting by mothers or fathers Values held by poor, lack of work ethic, commitment Breakup of families Addiction, mental illness, domestic violence	Lack of employment Lack of education Inadequate skill sets Decline in neighborhoods Big government Decline in social morality Urbanization Suburbanization of manufacturing Middle class flight Inelastic cities, inadequate regional planning Immigration Failure of social services Absence of knowledge, worker skills, intellectual capital Social capital Lack of career ladder between knowledge and service sectors Speed of economic transformation at local level	Minimum wage versus living wage Temporary jobs Less than 30 hours/week Lack of benefits Disposable employees Debt bondage Global outsourcing Payday lenders Lease/purchase Redlining Drug trade Exploitation for markets Exploitation of resources and raw materials The intersection of classism and other "-isms": sexism, racism, heterosexism, ageism	Policies that result in economic and social disparity Undue influence of corporations on legislation Tax structure that shifted tax burden to middle class, away from wealthy and corporations Decline in wages for bottom 90% Decline of unions De-industrialization Management/ labor "bargain" CEO to line worker salary ratio Profit-/financial-centered form of globalization

Adapted from *Bridges Out of Poverty: Strategies for Professionals and Communities Workbook* (2006)

Poverty Research Continuum

CAUSES	Behaviors of the Individual	Absence of Human and Social Capital	Human Exploitation	Political/ Economic Structures
ASSUMPTIONS	By studying the poor, we will learn what changes individuals must make in order to climb out of poverty. The poor are somehow lacking, either because of their own bad choices or because of circumstances. They should become "like us." Poverty is a sustainable condition.	By studying human and social capital, we will learn how to work within the larger political/ economic structure to create conditions that foster prosperity. Faith that the market and market corrections will create most of the conditions necessary for general prosperity. Acceptance of a 4–5% unemployment rate as a normal feature of the economy.	By studying colonial and imperialist behavior, we can learn how to create just and equitable economic structures. Dominant groups discount the legitimacy of this category and look to the future. Dominated people (Appalachian, African-Americans, Native Americans, former colonies) remember the past and may seek redress.	Studying the poor is not the same thing as studying poverty. Race, class, and gender are categories for analysis, not just demographics.
WHAT'S SAID	Don't blame the system; change the individual. Don't upset the system.	Don't blame the political/ economic system; change the individual and the community system.	Upset the system and make it fair.	Don't blame the individual. Change the political/ economic structure; fight poverty instead of reforming welfare.

Adapted from *Bridges Out of Poverty: Strategies for Professionals and Communities Workbook* (2006)

Poverty Research Continuum

CAUSES	Behaviors of the Individual	Absence of Human and Social Capital	Human Exploitation	Political/ Economic Structures
STRATEGIES	Hold individual accountable and use sanctions if necessary Target individuals Work First programs Self-sufficiency Enhance language experience Psychology of mind Treatment interventions Resiliency Work ethic Mentors Literacy Asset development Marriage promotion Caseload reductions All strategies focus on the individual	Hold individual and social service systems accountable Use sanctions if necessary Full employment, growth in labor market Education Skill development Anti-poverty programs for childcare, child support, healthcare, and housing EITC (Earned Income Tax Credit) Regional planning Community action programs Head Start Workforce Investment Act Continuous growth One-stop centers	Hold the exploiters accountable Educate all people about the power differentials within the community Create an action plan to address the exploitation Community-based development Political organizing to win control over economic and political institutions	Hold political/ economic power structure accountable Use economic disparity trends as a measure Interdisciplinary approach to macroeconomic planning and policies Whole-system planning Enhance living standards Redistribution of wealth in other direction Access to capital and ownership

Adapted from *Bridges Out of Poverty: Strategies for Professionals and Communities Workbook* (2006)

Understanding these four areas of research on poverty will be a great asset to you as you advance in your career in law enforcement.

When you first begin your work in law enforcement, most of your time is spent dealing directly with people. The previous chapters were intended to share understanding and tools you can use when working directly with people from different economic communities. As you become a senior officer and/or get promoted, the department will often require that your focus shift from individual interactions to a more systemic viewpoint, and you will be required to work effectively within the system. The systems that allow the poverty you have worked with to continue will now be the main things you and your staff will deal with. The department will call on you to work not only directly with individuals, but also with other organizations within the community and with the community at large—maybe even at the policy level.

Receiving promotions or becoming a senior officer generally means that you will be called to do more work with entire communities and outside agencies. In order to be effective, it will be helpful if you can identify within the four major causes of poverty the one that interests you the most, and then identify the primary areas of interest of those with whom you are called to work. This will allow you to engage people where they are, rather than reacting judgmentally to views that are different from your own.

Poverty has always been with us. Researchers have worked hard to try to identify the causes of poverty, not only because serving the poor takes resources, but because too much poverty can actually affect a community's and a country's stability. Therefore, if we understand all the causes of poverty, we will be able to create a holistic solution, one that doesn't simply focus on one cause, but initially addresses all of the causes.

BEHAVIORS OF THE INDIVIDUAL

The first area of research on poverty is focused on studying the behaviors of the individual in poverty. We study "Fred" in poverty. We look at Fred and his behaviors and conclude that they are the reason (or are the main contributors to) why Fred is in poverty. We research such topics as single parenthood, substance abuse, work ethic, and anything else that has to do with the individual's choices and attitude. We say things like, "This person drinks too much, and that's why he is in poverty. Too many people are single parents; that's why there is poverty. Fred in poverty has a poor work ethic; that's the cause of poverty."

One of the assumptions underlying this area of research is that by studying the poor we will learn what new behaviors individuals will have to learn so they can pull themselves out of poverty. Strategies or solutions that are a direct result of this area of research are programs like Work First. Surely if Fred gets a job, then he will be out of poverty; therefore, create a Work First program, and never mind that the job Fred obtains does not pay a livable wage, that is not the focus. Fred is working—that is the point. The research focused on Fred, so the solution will depend on Fred. Do you see solutions in the communities in which you work that are strictly based on the individual? There is a good chance that they are products of the research done regarding the behaviors of the individual.

HUMAN AND SOCIAL CAPITAL IN THE COMMUNITY

The second area of research on poverty is human and social capital within the community. Here there is a focus on factors within the community that cause poverty. That Fred is in poverty is not just due to Fred; the community in which Fred lives is the main contributing factor that keeps him in poverty. Research will show that poverty communities often have less livable wage jobs, test scores are often lower in schools, zoning laws are different, and funding is not the same. Therefore, the solutions are community-based. Get local businesses to pay a livable wage, and we will end poverty. Make the school system produce stronger results, and we will end poverty.

Robert Putnam writes in his book *Bowling Alone* about human and social capital declining in many of America's neighborhoods—not just in poverty—meaning we don't know our neighbors and are therefore less likely to assist each other. Community groups, lodges, clubs, and leagues are declining in membership. One role these organizations played was to ensure that communities knew each other and cared for each other. From a community not providing livable wage jobs to the decline in social capital that Putnam writes about, this area of research focuses on the community and how factors therein contribute to the causes of poverty.

HUMAN EXPLOITATION

The third area of research focuses on exploitation of people and communities. This area of research concludes that as long as individuals and communities are treated differently based on economic background, gender, race, age, and/or sexual orientation, then there will continue to be poverty. The fact that classism (the belief that because you come from a certain class you have different abilities) exists is one of the main causes of poverty. This area of research will often focus on naming the exploitation and solving the problem by raising awareness of the exploitation, examining how the exploitation affects everyone (not just those being exploited), and calling for a particular action. Robert Jensen's book *The Heart of Whiteness* is a great example of someone clearly naming an exploitation, analyzing how it has affected him and the group of people he represents, and calling for action. Exploitation can be very complicated as it can occur in many ways to numerous people. For example, one person might experience the "benefits" of being part of the dominant gender group while simultaneously being exploited due to age, race, or any other factor. Therefore, the focus of this area is not to point the finger at just one group and place blame; rather, it is to name the ways in which one group of people wields more power than another group because of its class, gender, race, age, sexual orientation, etc., to analyze the negative effects for everyone (not just those who are being exploited), and to call all parties to a direct action.

POLITICAL AND ECONOMIC STRUCTURES

The fourth and final area of research focuses on political and economic structures. This area focuses on city, county, state, and federal policies that favor one economic class over another. Researchers here will study which group of people has the most influence on legislators and the resulting policies that are passed. It researches how the tax structure is set up and points to the people/entities it benefits most. The solution here, in contrast to the solution posed by the first area of research, focuses on creating fair economic and political systems. The focus is on the system, not on the individual.

In his book *Wealth and Democracy,* Kevin Phillips analyzes the wealthy class and how policies and political influence have helped the wealthy maintain their wealth and become wealthier throughout America's history. Though the book examines some individuals, the focus is on how those individuals' actions influenced political and economic structures to favor the wealthy, often at the expense of the middle class and those in poverty.

FINDING YOUR FOCUS AND UNDERSTANDING OTHER VIEWS

Many people develop a "favorite" area of research, meaning one that they feel has a greater impact than the others. Most people also have a "least favorite" area of research, one they don't believe has as much legitimacy as the others. It's my guess that as you read about the four areas of research, one in particular clicked with you and made you think, "Yeah, that's it! That's what causes poverty." That area of research may well be the one you will (or already have) come to emphasize. This cause of poverty and the solutions that stem from it will be easy for you to discuss with other people. However, as you become a senior officer, it is likely that you will be called to work with many partners, all of whom will have their own favorite areas as well. In order to be effective within these community meetings, you will need to be aware of what your favorite area of research is and be able to identify what areas of research are most interesting to others.

Within a given community, those who favor the causes that fall under the individual behavior category will often find themselves polarized against those who favor causes related to political and economic structures. One group is saying poverty is caused by the individual, and the other group is saying that poverty is caused by the system. As a high-ranking member of the law enforcement community, you will be called upon to address causes that fall under all of these categories. In fact, it is imperative that any community working to reduce poverty address all four areas if it wishes to be effective.

> **TOOL:**
> All four areas of research will have to be addressed if a community wants to effectively reduce poverty. Be aware of your community partners' favorite areas of research when you work with them, but don't forget to be aware of your own preference as well.

All four areas of research are legitimate. Does Fred in poverty make individual choices? You better believe he does! Does the community influence those decisions? Certainly. We have all seen a child with potential get sucked into the criminal activities of the neighborhood. Is there exploitation? Any officer who has worked in both extremely wealthy and extremely poor neighborhoods can tell you about the different levels of access the two classes have because of their different levels of income. And we have all seen how political and economic structures have affected the neighborhoods we work with.

In his book *American Dream,* Jason DeParle shares the stories of three women from generational poverty. However, as he tells their stories, he also writes about the political and economic policies being drafted, passed, and implemented at the same time. Some of the policies meant to address poverty do not affect these women at all; some have a direct impact on them. Through the course of this book, DeParle makes it clear that every administration, whether Republican or Democratic, had its "favorite" area of research and put policies in place to address that area. But, in order to address poverty successfully, we will need to deal with all four areas of poverty during the same time period.

This means that both of the participants who raise their hands during my presentation—one stating loudly, "Poverty is all Fred's fault! If he would just get off his butt, get a job, and do what he has to do, then we wouldn't have poverty!" and the participant in the next seat exclaiming just as loudly, "It is *not* Fred's fault! If there were more fair trade than free trade, we wouldn't have lost all our decent-paying factory jobs. If lobbyists funded by the rich didn't have so much influence, then we wouldn't have poverty! Political and economic structures cause it!"—both of these participants have legitimate arguments, and both will have to be listened to and addressed if we are ever going to decrease or eliminate poverty.

Knowing the area of research you relate to most is essential to working effectively within a community. Understanding what areas the other participants favor and being able to understand their viewpoints is crucial. Being able to bring everyone to the table and make them feel that their points are legitimate while honoring their neighbors' viewpoints will cause you to be viewed as an effective leader. That makes your job easier and your department's public image more favorable.

LAW ENFORCEMENT LEADERSHIP: APPLYING THIS MATERIAL IN THE DEPARTMENT AND IN SOCIETY AT LARGE

This information can be useful for law enforcement officials throughout their careers. There are four areas in which officers can use this information: within individual interactions, within the departments or institutions for which they work, within the communities in which they work and live, and within the area of policy-level decisions. As we discussed in earlier chapters, an officer's career often begins with a lot of direct contact with individuals from different economic backgrounds. The previous chapters are meant to help officers better understand the complex ways in which economic class influences people and their actions. Armed with this understanding, an officer can choose his/her next response, rather than just react. Reacting often means the officer is no longer in control, and that is dangerous. Understanding what is happening in front of you allows you to choose what the next move is. This allows an officer the opportunity to be viewed as a good leader. Being viewed as a good leader gets you respect in the community and ultimately makes the job easier.

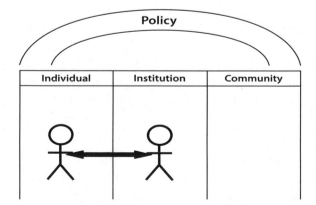

Using this information at the individual level alone is often insufficient, especially after one has been promoted to a senior position. To gain the most from this information, a law enforcement worker will want to apply it in all four areas. If we do not implement this information at the departmental, community, and policy levels, we will not change the system or the community; therefore, law enforcement personnel who come after you will continue to face the same or even greater challenges. In order to have a long-term effect, this information must be used within all four areas.

APPLICATION WITHIN LAW ENFORCEMENT ORGANIZATIONS

At times I hear officers state that they try to take the time to build more relationships with individuals within the different communities, but the department does not support their efforts. These officers are caught in a triangle with their departments and the individuals they serve, and most times it is the departments that dictate acceptable interactions between officers and citizens. This information must be used within the institution or department as much as it is used with individuals. Begin to think about how this information can be used during the training of new cadets, during the hiring process, and in the way the department operates. For example, who created the questions for hiring? Were they generated by personnel who are from one class? If a person from wealth wrote all of the questions in the interview, would a person from wealth or middle class have an unfair (yet unnoticed) advantage when answering them? Some departments have integrated this information into the training in the police academy as a way to prepare their officers. Oth-

99

er departments have used the information (especially this last chapter) to prepare their officers when moving from a focus on individual interactions to a focus on community and/or systemic issues.

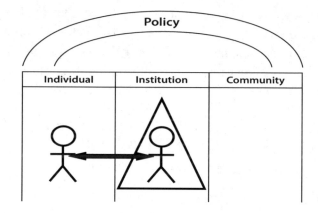

APPLICATION IN THE COMMUNITY

The events that occur within the community absolutely affect the department, as well as the officers' individual interactions. Officers can attest to the positive results of access to numerous livable wage jobs, banking institutions, green spaces, activities for youth, and schools with strong funding and low student-teacher ratios. These are just some of the things that, whether present or absent in a community, will influence law enforcement. Research shows a direct link between the number of kids who drop out of school and criminal activity in the future. Some places use school test scores to predict how many new prison units they will need. Law enforcement has, over time, seen its role within the community as a crucial one, and in many of our communities you will see officers in schools participating in after-school programs, assisting with fund raising, as well as doing community policing. As officers implement this information within the community, it will become clear that policies guide and influence what is possible within the community.

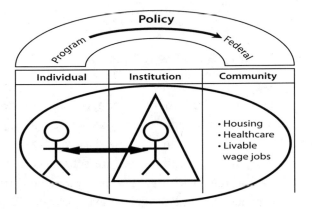

APPLICATION AT THE POLICY LEVEL

The fourth and final way to implement this information is by reviewing polices. This includes policies of the department, the city, the county, all the way up to federal policies. Policies directly and indirectly influence departments and individual interactions. Think about the policies many states have put in place regarding pseudoephedrine and how that has affected the illegal production of methamphetamine. Begin to think about how the information in the previous chapters can be used to shape policies within the department and at the city and state levels. Again, go back to the policies that regulate hiring: Are any of them geared toward one class more than another?

In order to utilize this material to the fullest, one will want to view this book through all four of the lenses: individual, department, community, and policy. To use this book solely to assist with individual interactions may help an officer in the present, but it will do little for the department and community in the long term.

INCREASING SELF-AWARENESS AND OWNING YOUR EXPERIENCE

The second objective of this mental model is to become aware of what your personal experience of the societal system has been. Law enforcement officers who are viewed as good leaders in all the different economic communities are often aware of their experience within the societal system and understand that the people they manage have had different experiences. When you own your personal experience of the system, then you can come to the table and teach others, as well as learn from those who have had different experiences.

A societal system includes these four major components: individuals, institutions, communities, and policies. It may have other elements, but these four major components must be present. Societal systems almost always operate in such a way that one group becomes normalized while others do not. By "normalized" I mean that the norms of one group are assumed to be the norms of society at large. Sometimes this happens unintentionally; sometimes it is very intentional. If you are part of the normalized group, you may be reaping benefits without even being conscious of it. In order to be the most effective leader, you will have to become aware of what your experience of the societal system has been, be willing to own it, and then be willing to come to the table and work with others who have had different experiences.

Let's use an example to further break down this point: When I present this material to an audience, I ask them to raise their hands if they are left-handed. (In the interest of full disclosure, I should note that I learned this activity from the Minnesota Collaborative Anti-Racism Initiative.) Then I ask the left hand-ed-folks, "Has our societal system normalized left-handedness or right-handedness?" The audience always responds, "Right-handedness!"

I continue: "If our societal system normalizes right-handedness, and if you are right-handed like me, then we should expect to find some things that are geared toward us, some benefits we receive simply because we are right-handed. What are some things that are geared toward right-handed people?" Answers such as notebooks, school desks, sporting equipment, kitchen utensils, door handles, credit card machines, and guns are fairly common. All of these are things that are made for people who are right-handed and have to be adjusted (or adjusted to) if the user is left-handed. I have presented this material for years, and every year people mention new things that have been designed for me as a right-handed person that I have never noticed. But the main point is that I didn't have to notice. The societal sys-tem has normalized right-handedness. I am right-handed, part of the normalized group, and therefore I receive benefits I am not aware of.

MIDDLE CLASS: THE AMERICAN NORM?

Apply this example to class. We have normalized middle class in America. I have asked families of four making approximately $19,000 a year what class they are in, and they responded, "Middle class." I asked families of four in the same region making more than $150,000 a year what class they are in, and the response was, "Middle class." Middle class is the class that many Americans want to be a part of. It is possible then that there are benefits people in middle class may receive simply because they are in middle class. Look again at the hidden rules of language and ask yourself which hidden rules and which register of language are most often used in schools, banks, businesses, and law enforcement. Middle class rules and formal register are most prevalent; thus, one who grows up in middle class has a built-in advantage when navigating those systems. This is a benefit to that person whether that person realizes it or not.

Many people have, in at least one area of their lives, experienced the benefits of being part of the norm, while in still another area they are not part of the norm. Kirby Moss writes about this very point in his book *The Color of Class: Poor Whites and the Paradox of Privilege*. As a man who is very well-educated and making a higher than average income, he talks about the benefits he has. Still, as a man of color, there are situations in which he does not experience the benefits of being part of the normalized group. For example, when he happens to be the only person of color in a working class bar in a primarily white town, the situation does not allow him to enjoy the benefits of being well-educated and having a higher than average income. In this situation he is not part of the norm because his race trumps the benefits he may get from other areas.

It is important to become aware of your experience of the societal system and to move toward ownership of that experience. This is not an afternoon activity; it tends to be a lifetime journey. It is crucial to being an effective leader. Moving toward ownership often requires one to process different emotions. For example, sometimes left-handed people are full of emotion, even angry, when they begin to discuss the various things that are designed for right-handed people and that exclude the left-handed. Likewise, when unaware right-handed people hear these complaints, they too start to get emotional—they start to feel guilty. I have heard right-handed people say, "Oh, I never knew that! I'll make some calls and try to change it!" Both parties must move through their emotions in order to take ownership. Owning your experience can mean acknowledging that you have received benefits that may have been inaccessible to others based on societal norms, or acknowledging the difficulty of adjusting to a system in which you are not part of the norm.

Once both parties own their experiences within the societal system, we can set a table in the community where we will listen to those who have had different experiences of that same community. If I own my experience, and a man my age from my community starts to talk about what it is like to be a man in our community, I don't over-talk him. When I own my experience, I can say I don't know what it is like to be a man. That man gets to teach me. I don't respond out of my guilt over not knowing or out of my indignation at his perceived benefits; I listen and try to understand. If he owns his experience, then when I talk about what it is like to be a woman in this community, he listens.

When both parties own their experiences, they are more willing to listen to and learn from each other, and that is when a dialogue of mutual respect can take place. Establishing a dialogue of mutual respect will cause law enforcement personnel to be seen and treated as leaders. This type of leader receives the community's respect and trust. All of this will make the job easier, allow you to be more effective, and keep you safer.

CLASS: BRINGING EVERYONE TO THE TABLE

It is important to note that class is one of the last areas in which the normalized group has no problem telling the other groups what to do and how to do it. In other areas (such as race, gender, and age) it has become politically incorrect for the normalized group to tell the other groups what to do. For example, when the social service, medical, and criminal justice systems started new programs that targeted people from poverty, were there any people from poverty at the table during the creation of those programs? Or was it primarily one group of people from one class using their experience of the societal system to formulate solutions to the problem and then telling another group to conform to the conditions required by the solutions? As we discussed before, it is often ineffective for one person or group of people to tell another group what the problem and solution are without any input from the other groups involved.

The following are two examples that further illustrate this point. If a group of men came into a room full of women and told them, "Ladies, our men's group has put together a support group for you women because we understand that it's difficult to be a woman in America, and we want to tell you what it's like and support you," right away many women would start to laugh and think, "Yeah, I'm going to come to your support group just to see what you put together."

Very similarly, if a group of white people told a group of people of color, "Hey, we put together a support group for you because we understand there is still racism in our country, so come to our support group for you," again, many people of color might laugh and say, "Oh, we're going to come just to see what you put together." Still, we often have only middle class people at the table putting together programs for people in poverty, and we never think twice about it. Class is one of the last areas in which the normalized group, middle class people, still has no problem telling the "other" group, people in poverty, what their problems are and creating solutions for them without seeking any input from them. The solutions created in these conditions are based on the middle class experience of the societal system, which we now understand is very different from that of poverty or wealth. In the cases of other "-ism" areas (like gender, age, and race) this is viewed as politically unacceptable, if not an outright injustice. When addressing any "-ism," all people affected will need to be at the table to contribute to the solutions.

It is important to note that though this book is not designed to address all the "-isms" of the communities you serve (sexism, racism, ageism, heterosexism, etc.), it is in your best interest to continue to gain knowledge about these areas because you will deal with them (and their legacies) frequently.

This book contains information that can be used when working directly with people from different economic classes, within a department, or in a community at large. Use the pieces of this book that pertain to your job, but remember to come back to it as you become a senior officer, are otherwise promoted, or move to another department. Often the focus of the job begins to change the longer we've been at it. Career advancement in the field of law enforcement demands that people expand their view, that they move from the level of the individual to the level of the community, and finally that they move to a systemic point of view. Officers, whether police, sheriffs, correctional, or probation, almost always start their careers by working directly with citizens. It is as important to begin to use this information with a department or community as it is to use it with individuals. All uses will make the job easier, help you to be perceived as a leader, and ultimately keep you and your fellow officers safer— and that is what is most important to all the people around you who love you.

It is my hope that the information in this book will help make all of your interactions more successful. When we begin to understand that different communities have different economic realities, we can choose responses that respect those realities and keep us safe. Thank you for all that you do and face every day.

Berne, Eric. (1996). *Games People Play: The Basic Handbook of Transactional Analysis.* New York, NY: Ballantine Books.

Brito, Corina Solé & Gratto, Eugenia E. (Eds). (2000). *Problem-Oriented Policing: Crime-Specific Problems, Critical Issues, and Making POP Work, Volume 3.* Washington, D.C.: Police Executive Research Forum.

Covey, Stephen R. (1989). *The Seven Habits of Highly Effective People: Powerful Lessons in Personal Change.* New York, NY: Simon & Schuster.

DeParle, Jason. (2005). *American Dream: Three Women, Ten Kids, and a Nation's Drive to End Welfare.* New York, NY: Penguin.

DeVol, Philip E. (2006). *Facilitator Notes for Getting Ahead in a Just-Gettin'-By World: Building Your Resources for a Better Life* (Revised Edition). Highlands, TX: aha! Process.

DeVol, Philip E. (2006). *Getting Ahead in a Just-Gettin'-By World: Building Your Resources for a Better Life* (Second Edition). Highlands, TX: aha! Process.

DeVol, Philip E., Payne, Ruby K., & Dreussi Smith, Terie. (2006). *Bridges Out of Poverty: Strategies for Professionals and Communities* (Fourth Edition). Highlands, TX: aha! Process.

DeVol, Philip E., Payne, Ruby K., & Dreussi Smith, Terie. (2006). *Bridges Out of Poverty: Strategies for Professionals and Communities Workbook.* Highlands, TX: aha! Process.

Feuerstein, Reuven, et al. (1980). *Instrumental Enrichment: An Intervention Program for Cognitive Modifiability.* Glenview, IL: Scott, Foresman & Co.

Jensen, Robert. (2005). *Heart of Whiteness: Confronting Race, Racism, and White Privilege.* San Francisco, CA: City Lights Publishers.

Joos, Martin. (1967). "The Styles of the Five Clocks." *Language and Cultural Diversity in American Education.* 1972. Abrahams, Roger D. & Troike, Rudolph C. (Eds.). Englewood Cliffs, NJ: Prentice-Hall.

Kim, W. Chan & Mauborgne, Renée. (1997). "Fair Process: Managing in the Knowledge Economy." *Harvard Business Review, 75*(4), 65–75.

Lui, Meizhu, Robles, Bárbara, Leondar-Wright, Betsy, Brewer, Rose, & Adamson, Rebecca. (2006). *The Color of Wealth: The Story Behind the U.S. Racial Wealth Divide.* New York, NY: New Press.

McCall, Nathan. (1995). *Makes Me Wanna Holler: A Young Black Man in America.* New York, NY: Random House.

Miller, William R. & Rollnick, Stephen. (2002). *Motivational Interviewing: Preparing People for Change* (Second Edition). New York, NY: The Guilford Press.

Moss, Kirby. (2003). *The Color of Class: Poor Whites and the Paradox of Privilege.* Philadelphia, PA: University of Pennsylvania Press.

Pascale, Richard Tanner & Sternin, Jerry. (2005). "Your Company's Secret Change Agents." *Harvard Business Review, 83*(5), 72–81.

Payne, Ruby K. (2005). *A Framework for Understanding Poverty* (Fifth Revised Edition). Highlands, TX: aha! Process.

Payne, Ruby K. (2005). *A Framework for Understanding Poverty Workbook* (Second Edition). Highlands, TX: aha! Process.

Phillips, Kevin. (2003). *Wealth and Democracy: A Political History of the American Rich.* New York, NY: Broadway.

Putnam, Robert. (2001). *Bowling Alone: The Collapse and Revival of American Community.* New York, NY: Simon & Schuster.

"Table HINC-05. Percent Distribution of Households, by Selected Characteristics Within Income Quintile and Top 5 Percent in 2007." (2007). *Current Population Survey, 2008 Annual Social and Economic Supplement.* Retrieved October 8, 2008 from U.S. Census Bureau Website, http://pubdb3.census.gov/macro/032008/hhinc/new05_000.htm.

Jodi Pfarr, M.Div. is an author, speaker, trainer, and consultant for aha! Process, Inc. She formerly served as a certified critical debriefer for the St. Paul, Minnesota Police Department, and is well familiar with police culture and the daily challenges faced by police officers. More recently Pfarr carried out an aha! Process/City of St. Paul Police Department training project and subsequent interviews with law enforcement personnel both in St. Paul and in other areas. Those trainings and interviews provided much of the information contained in this book. Pfarr is currently the executive director of Emma Norton Services, where she helps provide housing to single women with low incomes. She resides in Minnesota.